Voices of Many Worlds

Malaysian Literature in English

Voices of
Many Worlds
Malaysian Literature in English

Fadillah Merican | Ruzy Suliza Hashim
Ganakumaran Subramaniam | Raihanah Mohd. Mydin

Times Editions

© **2004 Federal Publications Sdn. Berhad**
(General & Reference Publishing)
Published by Times Editions – Marshall Cavendish
An imprint of Federal Publications Sdn. Berhad (3024 -D)
(General & Reference Publishing)
A member of Times Publishing Limited

Times Subang
Lot 46, Persiaran Teknologi Subang
Subang Hi-Tech Industrial Park
Batu Tiga, 40000 Shah Alam
Selangor Darul Ehsan, Malaysia
Tel: (603) 56352191   Fax: (603) 56352706
E-mail: cchong@tpg.com.my

Singapore Office:
Marshall Cavendish International (Asia) Private Limited
Times Centre, 1 New Industrial Road,
Singapore 536196
Tel: (65) 62139288   Fax: (65) 62854871
E-mail: te@tpl.com.sg
Online Bookstore: http:/ /www. timesone.sg /te

National Library (Malaysia)   Cataloguing-in-Publication Data
Voices of many worlds: Malaysian literature in English/ Fadillah
          Merican ... [et. al.]
          Bibliography: p. 17
          ISBN 983-580-989-5
          1. Malaysian literature (English). I Fadillah Merican.
          899.2300805
Printed in Malaysia by BS Print (M) Sdn. Bhd.

Dedicated to
all writers and scholars of literature.

Acknowledgement

The creativity and scholarship of many people have made this project possible. We dedicate this book to all writers and scholars of the literature of this area and related fields.

We would like to thank Universiti Kebangsaan Malaysia for the grant which enabled us to undertake research into Malaysian Literature in English. We would like to extend our appreciation to the School of Language Studies & Linguistics (previously Faculty of Language Studies) and the Faculty of Social Sciences and Humanities of UKM for being supportive of our efforts.

Our gratitude and special appreciation go to our colleagues, especially those in the Literature Committee; friends from Malaysian universities and overseas; and the many students we have taught.

We thank you all for your interest, support, assistance and valuable dialogue. From our friendships and shared interests we have drawn vital personal sustenance.

Contents

Introduction
by Fadillah Merican

1.0 Epigraph

> [The] postcolonial canon is the numerous nodes of
> writing in English produced by local national writers,
> read perhaps only by their local national audiences,
> the entire rhizomous planet of minorities... replacing
> the hegemonic and hierarchical world view of the
> imperialists.

— Shirley Lim Geok-lin
(1994, p. 6)

1.1 Introduction

The voices of many worlds make up Malaysian literature in English. No contemporary discussion on any aspect of this body of literature can dispense with acknowledging the country's multicultural, multiethnic, multilingual complexity especially in the face of "young nation" status and nation building: Acknowledging the cultural, historical, political and physical milieu that has shaped and continues to shape the region's creative writing in English sets the broad parameters before discussions of a more specific nature can be carried out. The existence of different voices is therefore inevitable, and thankfully so, for their rich diversity and interrelatedness give depth and dimension to, what Sheryll Stodhard in the editor's introduction calls "the tessellated milieu of agendas, visions and revisions we call contemporary Malaysia" (1998, p. xv).

This book acknowledges these voices by highlighting the many worlds which make up Malaysian creative writing in English. It is hoped that in the individual chapters and from the book as a whole, the reader is provided with a comprehensive collection of works that are sometimes similar, sometimes overlapping and interrelated in content, style, effect or sometimes conflicting, resulting in works that can be so diverse in some aspects, yet similar in others.

We have considered the writers and their works without being slavish about procedure and without categorising and naming every "world" to which they belong. The readers will recognise many of them. There is the world of different ethnic origins of our writers— Malay, Chinese, Indian and Iban. Then there are the more specific cultural domains for example the Peranakan, the traditional Chinese community based on Confucian principles; the Tamil, the Sri Lankan communities of the Indian world; the Kelantan enclave in the Malay world; and the hybrid worlds of intercultural marriages cutting across fixed domains. Religious and spiritual practices provide crucial lifelines and other worlds. Then there are the socioeconomic systems with built-in structures and boundaries. Parameters of place and time provide an array of post-this and pre-that, of established and new, young and old, outsiders and insiders. There is the age-old world of gender and engendered differences, one that opens up new reading perspectives. Last but certainly not least, the world of literary and aesthetic influences from East and West resulting in intertextual resonances. The voices of these various worlds are not only those of the producers and the writers, but of the teeming, colourful, sad, joyous, harmonious and fractured individuals of the fictional world they create.

We would like to affect a shift of emphasis for viewing Malaysian literature in English in this book. Important, and oft-mentioned comments on the state of the art will be given their due recognition in the chapters of the book relevant to the concerns of specific writers. These include references to the beleaguered state of Malaysian writing in English, with the massive changes in national culture when English lost its status with the passing of the National Language Act in 1967. Then there are the references to the even greater marginalising of writing in English with the 1969 racial riots, the subsequent rise of Malay nationalism, and specific policies in the name of nation building and national culture which denied "national literature" status for any writing not in the national language. The lack of knowledge and commitment amongst younger writers of the "real" historical and cultural issues of the country is also seen as yet another obstacle to the flourishing of English writing in Malaysia and the dire straits it is in.

By concentrating on the productivity of each of the writers in the thirteen chapters and on new voices in the final chapter, we would celebrate the tenacity, quality and dogged spirit of Malaysian literature in English and its writers in spite of the "constraints", the "self-censorship" and the "marginalisation". Shirley Lim's comment on postcolonial literatures is particularly relevant to Malaysian literature in English. Her reference to "nodes" and "rhizomous planet of minorities" in the opening section of this chapter aptly capture the slow but steady, never-completely-spent energies of Malaysian literature in English. It is like an underground stem that produces roots and leafy shoots. A node on a branch signals the possibilities of new growth. If we stretch the image a little further, the nodal association of a meeting place of lines, roads or parts, we have a most fitting description of our literature in English. The words "local national writer" and "local national audiences" provide some affirmation that despite what has been written about the sorry condition of Malaysian literature in English, it still has a relevance that is "national" despite the use of the coloniser's language and "the absence of a common source of collective imagery".

Which brings us to the matter of homogeneity and heterogeneity. The absence, at this point in time, of "a common source of collective imagery, symbols and myths" is a result of history and our heterogeneous multiethnic and multicultural population, more so in a country that has had its fair share of fits and starts towards a common national identity let alone a cultural identity. In the 1940s and 1950s, in the face of the colonial presence and then later with the new-found independence, there was the quest for national identity and the belief that a genuinely original Malayan literature would carry the identity of the modern nation.

For those writing in Malay or English this fervent quest for a literature to express the national identity was made before that identity had been worked out. Dudley de Souza compares this with the case of the Philippines, which had already achieved a degree of cultural integration (via Catholicism) long before the 2nd World War through unity against a common enemy (the Spaniards) and a literature, particularly the novels of Rizal, that helped to pull the people together (Quayum & Wicks, 2001). It was also different from the case of Czechoslovakia and its revival in the early 19th century when translations of European works was part of an explicit cultural policy of selection and retaliation to combat further attempts to "denationalise" both the common people and the higher classes (Bassnett, 1993). In the 1940s and 1950s there was no national identity and today, into the new century, we are still working towards forging a shared identity collectively acceptable to the diverse peoples. What we have now and will continue to have is this heterogeneity. Instead of seeing the absence of a shared consciousness and identity as a problem to the healthy development of Malaysian literature in English, it is this diversity of cultures and cultural identity together in a shared landscape and context that we should celebrate. The different ethnic myths should not be seen as "divisive" but a rich store of resources from the Malaysian hinterland for writers to select and present, adapt and transform.

The diverse voices and the issues taken up in Malaysian creative writing in English have, for too long been regarded as separate, discordant, even recalcitrant articulations that do not contribute much to the nation-building, integration and a Malaysian identity. It is our belief that the diversity, the preoccupation with bleak scenarios and the reality of complex class divisions, social and cultural dislocations ironically represent a collective commitment towards highlighting differences to promote integration. This is very much a literature of reconciliation, offering various perspectives of the rocky path to nationhood. As part of the nation's discourse (together with other forms for example media, official communication, etc.) Malaysian creative writing reveals, in the art, the state of the culture. As Maznah Mohammad and Wong Sook Koon state in their introduction to *Risking Malaysia: Culture, Politics and Identity*:

> Historical studies may empirically relate events but perhaps only literature can heighten the representation of a lived experience; it may even be a medium more productive than committee reports for feeding into the reinvention of the future.
>
> (2001, pp. 31–32)

By choosing to write mainly of a specific community, as in the case of K. S. Maniam, Mohammad Haji Salleh, Che Husna Azhari and Wong Phui Nam, a writer is not lacking in a balanced and Malaysian sensitivity. Some of the best "communally-centred" works rise above narrow community concerns to acknowledge implicitly and explicitly, the larger (national) context of diverse groups, multicultural relations and the difficulties of achieving meaningful intercultural communication. All of these works are facets of the Malaysian reality. At the very least they enable Malaysians to know and consider the beliefs, the conflicts, dreams and hang-ups of the other communities in the neighbourhood and to realise whilst there are differences, there are also similarities.

The numerous "nodes" of writing in English in Malaysia surely belong to one branch. From its early beginnings in the 1940s with dedicated pioneers such as Wang Gungwu, Ee Tiang Hong, and Wong Phui Nam, to the present, with its slew of new writers, there is a substantial and growing body of Malaysian works in English. The positive attitude towards English and the moves taken to realise new (or renewed) goals for English in the educational sector, are hopeful signs for the nurturing of creative writing in English. The publication of anthologies of creative writing and of critical essays will help strengthen the industry. There is also increased activity in the translation of Malay works into English; an example is Salleh ben Joned's translation of Latiff Mohidin's poems (2003).

Lately, there have been posthumous publications of writers who have passed on. Landmark Books has published *No Visitor's Allowed*, a collection of short stories by John Machado; and the Maya Press' publication of Lee Kok Liang's *London Does Not Belong to Me*. Both these publications are a welcome addition to the corpus as are new works by established writers, for example, K. S. Maniam's *Between Lives* (2003).

Increased interest and research in Malaysian literature in English are logical expectations feeding in their turn the production of creative writing. No less important is the infrastructure offered by universities. Programmes and courses offering postcolonial literatures, on specifically Malaysian literature in English provide continuity of interest, writing about and producing for Malaysian creative writing in English. Possibilities for research are many.

One of the largest categories would be studies that are comparative in nature. This could be at the intra-level of Malaysian writers writing in English, at the national level, between languages, and at the level of crossing physical and linguistic boundaries—international works from Southeast Asia, Asia and other parts of the world. The discussions could use a range of approaches—interdisciplinary, genre, influence, thematic and translation studies.

As postcolonial writing, the corpus is rich in aspects of culture, politics and identity. Cultural studies could tap into areas such as cultural identity, of construction and reconstruction, of race relations, of the politics of language, of modernity and globalisation. Various aspects of the Malay identity could be explored, for example Malay politics, Malay women, Malays and modernity, and "Melayu Baru". The works of Karim Raslan, Che Husna Azhari, Mohammad Haji Salleh and Lloyd Fernando could offer a variety of representations. The huge body of literary works in Malay provides many possibilities for comparative topics ranging from racial relations to literary influences. The involvement of young novelists, for example, Faisal Tehrani in drama, broadens the corpus of works and bodes well for comparative and cross-cultural investigations. Sociological studies of Malays and of Malaysia could be used to frame and strengthen arguments. The same holds true for various other communities in Malaysia.

Gender perspectives would be another rich area; one that cuts across comparative, postcolonial and cultural studies. Notions of male masculinity, female identity and agency for Malaysian women of specific ethnic communities and age groups would make interesting investigations. The writings of Malaysians abroad— transnational writers—who move between cultural boundaries, could be scrutinised for what is revealed or not revealed of a Malaysian consciousness; and of the audience the works are written for. Are they Malaysia-centred or merely Malaysia/Orient-based for a Western readership?

The recent volume of new writings in the form of short stories and plays could be examined for global and international relevance as opposed to local significance. Do the newest stories take up issues and shared problems of young men and women of a world without boundaries rather than those specifically Malaysia? Development-focused studies of various genres could be undertaken, with emphasis on specific periods of sociopolitical changes or upheavals.

Malaysianisation/nativisation of English in our creative writings provides a variety of linguistic strategies to consider. For all these areas for research, the use of a wide range of literary theories, from Marxist to reader response to postcolonial, will add dimension and focus to the discussions.

The selection of writers for these chapters is not exhaustive. We would have liked a chapter devoted exclusively to newer short stories; one for Ghulam-Sarwar Yousof for his contributions to Malaysian literature in English in the 1970s and 1980s, and his continuing support of the research in literature and the arts in Malaysia. It would have done Malaysian drama justice to have devoted a chapter on the development of Malaysian drama and theatre in English from the early post-war years, through independence, the lean years of the 1960s and mid-1970s, the gradual revival by the mid-1980s and the present active local and imported theatre scene. A chapter on the development of early Malaysian creative writing in English would pay tribute to the fraternity of pioneer poets such as Wang Gung Wu, Ee Tiang Hong, Omar Mohd. Noor, Lee Geok Lan and many others (Thumboo, 1973; 1976). Last but not least, a chapter devoted to English translations of source texts in Malay, Chinese and Tamil would have added to the corpus and alerted readers to the wealth of discussions that can arise from comparative studies of literary translations.

However, we are confident that the writers covered in the present chapters are important voices—as critics, personalities in the arts and most important of all, as orchestrators of other voices in the innumerable texts and contexts they have created. They have been chosen as literary pioneers at home and abroad, new voices of the 1970s and 1980s and even newer ones of the 1990s and the new millennium. Read together, the accounts of their work will provide a comprehensive, more detailed picture of the sociopolitical conditions and emotional landscape of the country better than any survey-type account could ever provide.

Literary works thrive and multiply in an environment of support, appreciation and scholarship. In recent years, there has been a noticeable development in academic research and the publication of critical writings and comparative studies on Malaysian literature in English. In 2001, Mohammad A. Quayum and Peter Wicks' *Malaysian Literature in English: A Critical Reader*, set in motion the publication of other volumes of critical essays and anthologies of short stories, poetry and plays. The Bibliograpahy at the end of this chapter, together with references to recent titles in the Bibliography of other chapters will, we hope, provide a comprehensive listing of new reference texts on the subject. We have thought it best to have a bibliography for each specific writer, to help readers with reference work although this will result in the inevitable repetition of entries for certain books.

The chapters on the specific writers share a common plan even if writing styles differ between the four researchers. The chapter components are: firstly, a fitting epigraph; secondly, an introduction that provides the writer's biography, crucial works, a brief but comprehensive summary of the influences and significant highlights of his or her life, the main thematic concerns and the writer's contribution to Malaysian literature in English; and thirdly, the heart of the chapter, the discussion of the writer's works. Given the nature of the writer's concerns, his/her corpus and the availability of texts, the structuring of this part is left to the particular researcher. This is followed by a short conclusion and the bibliography.

In our discussion of works, reference will also be made to important studies on the writer and the writer's work. It is hoped the references to these critical essays will prove useful to the serious researcher. In many cases we have not mentioned all the critical essays available but the secondary references section in the bibliography for each chapter will list the titles deemed useful for reference.

The chapters are arranged chronologically taking the year of the writer's first significant publication as a guide. This will allow for a more continuous, sequential unfolding of the Malaysian landscape as we begin with Ee Tiang Hong whose first publication was in 1960, and end with the exciting new voices of Malaysian literature in English in its national and international contexts of Malaysia in 2003.

In the way we have set out the chapters and in highlighting possible areas for research and interesting facets of the subject, we sincerely hope that this book will be informative to both readers new to the area of study, and the more serious explorers of the subject—teachers, lecturers and university students of literature and related disciplines, and possibly future writers of Malaysian literature in English.

Bibliography

Primary Texts

Ghulam-Sarwar, Y. (1982). *Perfumed memories*. Singapore: Graham Brash.

————. (1982). *Halfway road, Penang*. Penang: Teks Publishing.

Lee, K. L. (2003). *London does not belong to me*. Petaling Jaya: Maya Press.

Maniam, K. S. (2003). *Audrey's promise*. Petaling Jaya: Maya Press.

————. (2003). *Between lives*. Petaling Jaya: Maya Press.

————. (2003). *Escape from module H 7953*. Petaling Jaya: Maya Press.

————. (2003). *Poison pen*. Petaling Jaya: Maya Press.

————. (2003). *Steel finger*. Petaling Jaya: Maya Press.

————. (2003). *Strange journey*. Petaling Jaya: Maya Press.

————. (2003). *The dragon lives again*. Petaling Jaya: Maya Press.

————. (2003). *The lost boys*. Petaling Jaya: Maya Press.

————. (2003). *The man who understood rocks*. Petaling Jaya: Maya Press.

————. (2003). *The treasure trunk*. Petaling Jaya: Maya Press.

————. (2003). *The well*. Petaling Jaya: Maya Press.

Salleh ben Joned. (2003). *Fables of dawn*. (Latiff Mohidin, Trans.). Petaling Jaya: Maya Press.

————. (2003). *Nothing is sacred*. Petaling Jaya: Maya Press

Spirit of the keris: A selection of Malaysian short stories and poems. (2003). Petaling Jaya: Maya Press (with Majlis Peperiksaan Malaysia).

Thumboo, E. (1973). *Seven poets*. Singapore: Singapore University Press.

————. (1976). *The second tongue. An anthology of poetry from Malaysia and Singapore*. Singapore: Heinemann Educational Books (Asia) Ltd.

Vethamani, M. E. (Compiler). (2003). *In-sights: Malaysian poems*. Petaling Jaya: Maya Press.

Machado, J. (2003). *No visitors allowed*. Singapore: Landmark Books.

Secondary Texts

Amir Muhammad, Karim Raslan & S. Stothard. (1998). *Generation: A collection of contemporary Malaysian ideas.* Kuala Lumpur: Hikayat Press.

Bassnett, S. (1993). *Comparative literature: A critical introduction.* London: Blackwell.

De Souza, D. (2001). The Poets of Malay[an] literature in English., *Malaysian literature in English. A critical reader.* M. A.Quayum & P. Wicks (ed.). Petaling Jaya: Pearson Education Malaysia. (pp.2–12)

Lim, S. G. (1994). *Writing Southeast Asia in English: Against the grain* London: Skoob Books

Maznah Mohamad & Wong, S. K. (2001). *Risking Malaysia: Culture, politics and identity.* Bangi, Selangor: Penerbit UKM.

Raihanah Mohd. Maidin & Shahrizah Ismail @ Hamdan. (ed.). (2003). *Linking literary identities: Malaysian society, culture and the other.* Serdang: Universiti Putra Malaysia Press.

Ruzy Suzila Hashim & Subramaniam, G. (eds.). (2003). *Reclaiming place and space: Issues in new literature.* Bangi, Selangor: Penerbit Universiti Kebangsaan Malaysia

Zawiah Yahya. (ed.). (2003). *Critical perspectives on Muhammad Haji Salleh.* Kuala Lumpur: Dewan Bahasa & Pustaka.

Suggested Reading

Fernando, L. (1997). *Cultures in conflict.* Singapore: Graham Brash.

Malachi, E. V. (2001). *Bibliography of Malaysian literature-English.* Petaling Jaya: Sasbadi Sdn. Bhd.

Mallari-Hall, L. J. & Tope, L. R. (1999). (eds.). *Texts and contexts: Interactions between literature and culture in Southeast Asia.* Quezon City, Philipines: University of the Philipines, Department of English and Comparative Literature.

M. Bakri Musa. (1999). *The malay dilemma revisited: Race dynamics in modern Malaysia.* Gilroy, California: Merantau.

Shamsul Amri Baharuddin. (ed.). (2001). *Social anthropology of the Malays: Collected essays of M6 swift.* Bangi, Selangor: Penerbit Universiti Kebangsaan Malaysia

Syed Husin Ali. (ed.). (1981). *Ethnicity, clan and development.* Kuala Lumpur: Persatuan Sains Sosial Malaysia.

Yamada, T. S. (ed.). (2002). *Virtual lotus: Modern fiction of Southeast Asia.* Ann Arbor: University of Michigan Press.

Zawiah Yahya. (1988). *Malay characters in Malaysian novels in English.* Bangi, Selangor: Penerbit Universiti Kebangsaan Malaysia.

Zawiah Yahya. (2002). Imagined realities: Nation-building through literature. *Tenggara 45/46,* (pp. 45–53.)

Ee Tiang Hong

1.0 Epigraph

> And though the elements
> sustain their pressure
> hard on the shoot
> and branches
> down to the root
> the great tree
> still upholds its versatility,
> safely, conveniently
> turning and twisting
> in every limb
> and fibre,
> and then resumes
> in some quiet hour
> its steadfast
> stature.

—*Tembusu* by Ee Tiang Hong
(Cited in Thumboo, 1976, p. 18)

1.1 Introduction

Ee Tiang Hong was born in Malacca in 1933 into a well-known Baba family. Malay, or Peranakan (the Baba variant of the Malay language) was his mother tongue. He grew up with the myths and mores of the Malay world. At the same time, even though he could not speak Chinese, the Chinese cultural strands remained in the core of values and beliefs, costumes, cuisine and festivals.

Like many of the older group of Malaysian writers in English, Ee was from the last generation to have been educated in English and to have seen so many political changes within a relatively short time. At the Tranquerah English High School where he had his primary education, Ee learnt English songs and rhymes; at the Malacca High School he was introduced to English poetry and the

Western literary and cultural heritage behind it. He was an avid reader, and the Japanese occupation, which brought access to Japanese stories, served to broaden his reading.

He began writing poetry in the 1950s when he was a student at the University of Malaya in Singapore. This was a time of post-war nationalism, of identity building and nationhood. He read English, history and philosophy. Together with other student leaders and academics such as his senior Wang Gungwu, Ee was involved with the "Engmalchin" project, which planed for the conscious transfer of appropriate local idioms (Malay, Chinese, Tamil and etc.) to basic English structure and lexis. In doing this, the usage of standard English would be liberalised and Malayan/Malaysian poets especially would be writing in the context of their own place, peoples and problems. "Engmalchin" did not succeed but Ee is deservedly known as a pioneer in the introduction of indigenous elements in Malaysian poetry, that is, the nativisation of English with its use of distinctively Malaysian-English expression, cultural and other local details from the Malaysian context.

Upon graduation Ee taught at school. His service record included being Vice-Principal, later Principal (Kota Bharu Teachers Training College) and Senior Education Officer, Ministry of Education. He resigned from government service in 1969, then lectured at the Faculty of Education, University of Malaya. Prior to 1975, Ee had published two collections of poems: *I of the Many Faces* (1960) and *Lines Written in Hawaii* (1973). In 1975, at forty-two, Ee immigrated with his family to Perth, Australia. This was the final result of a disillusionment with what he saw as the divisiveness in Malaysian society engendered by a political system that was organised along the ethnic lines and which politicised all issues of race, language, culture and religion. Ee felt he could neither operate nor contribute meaningfully and productively in an environment that prejudiced his right to speak as a Malaysian and a writer. In 1976, *Myths for a Wilderness* was published. In 1979, he was granted Australian citizenship. In 1984, he completed his Ph.D. at the University of Western Australia. His thesis was titled "Education in Malaysia and Singapore: A Comparative Study of Racial and Cultural Factors as determinants of Educational Policy 1945–1970." For many years he was a lecturer in Education at the Western Australia College of Advanced Education where he continued to write creatively. *Tranquerah* was published in Singapore in 1985. In 1990, he died of cancer.

Nearing a Horizon was posthumously published in 1994. Ee's poems have also appeared in journals such as *Focus* (the journal of the Literary Society of University of Singapore), *Tenggara* (journal of Southeast Asian Literature), *Westerly* and *Jam Seven*. His poems are also featured in various anthologies compiled by Edwin Thumboo, and in *The Anthology of Malaysian Poetry* compiled by K. S. Maniam and M. Shanmughalingham.

In the 1950s, the aftermath of the war, which brought socio-political changes to the country, coincided with Ee's under-graduate days. This was a time of nascent nationalism and heightened consciousness of politics and culture for Ee and his contemporaries. The proposal for "Engmalchin" was part of the speculation over the status and functions of English after Independence. Ee saw this as a liberating influence, a way to a mature view of language because it meant "losing political allegiance" to the Queen's English and a step towards nationalising the language and literature. "Engmalchin" failed because total commitment to a political poetic medium must have been difficult for young idealists to follow through, as they had been nurtured on English literature, Western liberal ideology and freedom of the artist. However, Ee's legacy is a collection of poems that is finely balanced in style, between the influence of an English literary heritage and his own multilingual, multicultural Malaysian heritage. Critics have written of Ee's ability for defamiliarisation (a process resulting from the use of English in a non-English environment), his use of local idioms and colloquialisms. (Holladay, 1985; Bennett, 1978).

Yet at the same time there is a restrained, quizzical, ironic native voice that is very much a part of Western literary tradition. Irony, humour, innuendo and allusion are Ee's stylistic tools. Thus, apart from the influence of Baba upbringing, his love for the English language and the powerful and liberating influence of English literature (including the emotive power and imagery of the Bible), the course of history and political events shaped the man and poet. Ee's voice carries clearly and consistently in his poems, a voice trained formally and informally by experiences of many worlds.

Of the Baba, Ee saw them to be "in reality the cultural mediation, the cultural exemplar of a natural integration of diverse cultures, not a simple admixture of cultures, still less a carbon copy of any one of them". On the personal level he stated, "And so, in as much as I count my English education a blessing, I am also proud of my Chinese biological cultural inheritance and the Malay cultural elements that are also inseparable from my total self." It was with pride that Ee acknowledged the Baba as "a prototype of the multicultural Malaysian drawing strength from many cultural springs" (1998, p. 28).

Apart from the multicultural education of a Baba upbringing, Ee acknowledged gratitude to teachers who taught him English, and later, English Literature at secondary school. In terms of "impact" and "liberating influences" he mentioned the poetry of William Wordsworth and Shelley for "their philosophical themes and the universal sweep of their concerns." He regarded education through literature as a "great liberator" able to "break down the barriers between people." He firmly believed that educational and literary enterprise "must tend towards the multicultural, towards a sense of a common humanity to be of any worth. The methods, the organisational arrangements and literary devices assume significance only as they advance these universal goals" (1988, p. 31).

Ee was disillusioned over what he saw as the increasing political bias against true multiculturalism and a real democracy "that lives in the stomach, as in the heart and head of every Malayan." Among other things, the "orientation and aspiration" of writing in English and non-Malay writers became suspect and peripheralised. The final turning-point of the influence of politics on Ee was the May 13 riots. Ee saw the constitutional changes made in the wake of the 1969 clashes as further confirmations of the marginalisation of non-Malays in the country. He held on to his belief that the Setapak Declaration of May 1965, of a Malaysian Malaysia (representing the voices of the opposition parties of all the constitutional states of the Federation) as the only workable meaning of Malaysia. Yet the political stand was part of a deeply felt liberal-humanist personal philosophy of life. The interrelatedness of political events and ideological moves on Ee as both ordinary citizen and writer is stressed again and again in his essay:

> I left Malaysia when I could no longer accept intellectually or emotionally, the official and Malay definition of the Malaysian nation and culture. And because the gap in our perceptions was so wide as to make negotiation impossible, I was convinced that I had no place in the new order of things, and not just as a writer but even as an ordinary citizen.

(1988, p. 36)

Thus, a Peranakan upbringing, an education on colonial lines, a knowledge of literary heritages and a love of literature in all its multicultural facets, deep faith in the liberating influence of literature through education and the politics and history of the times combined to influence the man, poet and his poetry.

1.2   Discussion of works

Ee's volumes of poetry comprise *I of the Many Faces* (1960), *Lines Written in Hawaii* (1973), *Myths of the Wilderness* (1976), *Tranquerah* (1985) and *Nearing a Horizon* (1994). His poems have appeared in many journals and anthologies of poems; for example those edited by Edwin Thumboo (1973; 1976). The poems, read together with his essays (see Bibliography) provide yet another dimension to the variegated tapestry of Malaysian literature in English. In this case, the body of works is that of a seventh generation Chinese of Baba heritage, a corpus that spans 50 years, and the poems of the last two collections belonging to the Australian part of Ee's life though still very much concerned with Malaysia.

Ee's poetry is the creative output of a member of a specific ethnic group in Malaysia—of the 1950s, 1960s and early 1970s—and as a result of that, of his political commitments. At the same time, the poetic strategies he employs are drawn from a mixed bag of influences: material from his socio-cultural milieu and the adoption of particular devices of style and presentation learnt from early exposure to English literature and the vast resources of the literary traditions behind its study.

The interlacing of personal biography, culture, history and politics consistently manifests itself in Ee's poetry. Much of the critical writing on Ee's poetry emphasise this; drawing attention to the inhospitable conditions for a non-Malay Malaysian, and for artistic activities not in Bahasa Malaysia. Ee's personal concerns, the outcome of strongly felt feelings over the socio-political environment he was in, which he felt marginalised non-Malays, are also the concerns of his poetry. He started writing in 1951, a time when multicultural Malaya was reshaping itself politically, socially, economically and intellectually for a new phase of development—looking out towards independence from British rule, and towards nation-building.

The poems relentlessly document Ee's dissatisfactions over social, political, cultural situations, conditions and conflicts. These interlace to foreground the poet himself (for the autobiographical note is strong), caught in the public repercussions of intensely felt personal convictions. A connecting thematic thread holds Ee's poems together from those in *I of the Many Faces* written in the 1950s to *Nearing a Horizon* (1994). This is the emphasis on the sense of alienation and dislocation felt by the poet, a Malaysian-Chinese caught in the political social changes of the times. The dislocation operates at a different level but is "all aspects of exile as a state and of the exile as a being (Singh, 1988, p. 226). This concern manifests itself in a number of recurrent situations and issues in Ee's poems. The subsequent analysis of Ee's poems will focus on these situations and issues or sub-themes. By considering the development of the sub-theses in light of the specificities of time and place that operated for Ee as seen in his volumes a broad chronological procedure will be adopted. For example, the poems in *Tranquerah* (published ten years after his immigration to Australia) are more retrospective in nature, the landscape built out of a poet's physical and poetic re-living and revisiting of old haunts and old situations.

Despite Ee's belief that the poet be true to his art and to himself, the impetus behind his poetry is his awareness and his articulation of what he saw as imperfections around him. Ee's poetry is often described as responsible, socially-committed poetry, writing with a moral stance, as persona frustrations at a social, political intellectual ills are given a public airing. It is generally believed by many critics that his later volumes of poems from the 1970s on and the physical severing of ties as a result of his emigration, provided the emotional distance and "the freedom to express himself truly, without fear of favour (Singh, 1988, p. 229). However, Ee's poetry, early or later, is clearly moral in tone, consistently living up to his perception of the role of the poet. Indeed the very issues that he takes up are reflected in his perception that the poet "would do well to be himself" and strive to enrich the life of his reader, to make it more enlightened, more sensitive, more compassionate:

> [The] writer cannot defer to the dictates of his public
> without short changing himself, and as a by-product
> short changing the public as well.
>
> (Cited in Thumboo's foreword to Ee Tiang Hong's
> *Myth for a Wilderness*, 1976, p. xii)

At the same time Ee believed that there is a time and place for every conceivable role of the writer and that:

> [A] road to liberation, to the fullest development of the self, begins with the knowledge of self not in splendid isolation . . . but in social interaction. The personal motivation, the inner impulse, will still be creative, tapping the resources of language and culture to enhance one's awareness of self and the environment. But the social determinant will become more pressing, and the resultant stance will then take on a political and educational edge—to speak with other people in an exchange of experience.

(1988, p. 21)

As mentioned earlier, a useful starting point to discussing the thematic concerns of Ee's poetry would be to consider Ee's sense of frustration, displacement and alienation as the given condition behind the motivation to record the differing degrees of dislocation he felt over time, and over situations, decisions and changes going on in the country. Over the years, although the emphasis would vary in the specific subject areas of focus, the preoccupation would always be with the injustices of politics and power and their effect on ordinary Malayans/Malaysians, particularly the immigrant Chinese minority. Proclaiming the fears, disillusionment and disgust, in varying degrees of sadness and anger, is the ironic, often restrained narrator, more often than not the poet-narrator. He is both ordinary citizen, and self-proclaimed spokesman for people caught in a web of changes: sharply commenting and criticising, at times irritated at his own ineffectuality and occasionally giving up.

The subsequent reference and analysis of Ee's volumes of poetry will thus pay some attention to how the poems manifest variations in subject matter, emphasis and tone to show the extent of frustration or alienation of the narrator; attention will also be focused on poetic style. The strategies Ee adopts to present his thoughts and shape his poems will be highlighted, particularly his fusion of Western literary tradition and the nativisation of English with the colour, symbols, icons and language of the Malayan/Malaysian world.

A statement in 1971 provides a useful entry-point to Ee's early poems. At the same time it provides insight into his idealism and humanism:

> [T]he poet . . . is responsible only for his art and to himself . . . To these questions [of nationalism], would suggest that the writer has no part to play, not consciously and directly, anyway . . . it is not only the immediate society or circumstances he is concerned with, but the larger society of man, a society composed not only of Malays, Chinese and Indians but of the countless variety of people spread over all the breadth and corners of the world. The whole world is his fountain.
>
> (Lim, 1994, p. 110)

Ee's poetry does not address the "questions of nationalism" as in supporting state ideology but neither is his poetry on the "art for art's sake" tack. Certainly his poetry is not detached from social and political concerns for literary production is born of place, society and history. In the earlier collections therefore we have thematic concerns that revolve round manifestations of the gap between what should be and is, of what is promised and what achieved, of loss and change, of poverty, irresponsibility of those in power; politics and the common man. The anger and passion of the later collections may be less pervasive here, but there is the same emphasis on social, political and intellectual imperfections as noted by a sensitive, honest, but restrained intellectual. In short, the earlier poems record the dislocation felt by the exile, who has not even left his country.

Ee's early poems in his first collection reveal a moral concern with the discrepancy between word and deed, between the professed and what is actually achieved. His belief in the benefits of the multicultural, the diverse, is deeply felt. The poet's "sustenance" lies in writing from and for other people. There is the commitment to enlighten and raw attention to collective social ills specifically Malaysian but often times rising to concerns of people everywhere. These early poems are not marked by the deep sense of dislocation and anger of the later poems; nevertheless the frustration and ironic exposés are there of the abuses of politics and power and those charged with the responsibility of guarding the people's welfare. The effort to create a Malaysian consciousness— "to speak with other people in exchange of knowledge and experience"—is evident not just in the subject matter but also in the nativasation of landscape and language.

In "To . . . " there is condemnation of the hollow materialism and success-orientated priorities of life in Kuala Lumpur. However, despite the use of the word "stuff" and the mundane rhymes of the first two stanzas to emphasise the maladies caused by obsession with status and possessions, the repetitive listing of the symbols of success is also an acknowledgement of the tempting nature of these trappings, how easily one acquisition can lead to another:

>**To . . .**
>Do not think I regret
>Failing to go so far
>As Kuala Lumpur,
>Top post, prestige, bank account,
>Big car, big house, friends who count.
>
>Do not think I envy
>Such important people as make
>Great show:
>Top post, prestige, bank account,
>Big car, big house, friends who mount.
>Do not mock my drilling in the mud
>With hardly a prospect

In Sleepy Hollow.
Seeing the stuff they value
In the capital,
I do not envy.

(1960, p. 4)

In *Pariah*, although the narrator is not directly present, the same sense of self-serving opportunism and of political power is pervasive in the figure of the "lowly scavenger", who "along a narrowing road" feeds on political leftovers and handouts, and by so doing keeps the wheels of political abuse rolling. For the most part the persona in this collection of poems comes across as restrained, dignified, aware of moral discrepancies and filled with foreboding at what is happening. There is little "to applaud" or "to celebrate" but the "political and educational edge" to the personal motivation of writing is already present. Drought takes up the physical as well as the metaphoric condition of lack of water and of the absence of commitment to a people's growth. In the same way *Address* ironically captures the sense of misdirection of opportunities, of forgotten early promises made by those in power when the common man's support was needed.

Address
Riding on air in American car comfort
So big you will not even feel a stir,
Will you coxcomb ever bend again
To the wonder of the people?
Who remember how in the darkness of their slumber
You perched, flapping your wings on the stakes
To a crow struggling *fajar* in.

(1960, p. 3)

A number of poems foreground feelings of unease and foreboding arising from spiritual death. In *Dying*, there is reflection on the relentless; a lonely passage of time in *Bus Stop*; and the despair of living under the weight of "compressing layers of stagnation" as expressed in *Prayer*. The opening poem *I of the Three Monkeys* exposes the frustration of the man who is forced to pretend ignorance of injustices and discrepancies. Public conflicts have their effects on the individual and the helpless individual colludes in perpetuating injustices on the powerless. The frustration is controlled but the irony and anger directed at the self anticipates the disillusionment of later poems when the persona is frustrated because he makes so little difference. Finally in *Dead End* the poem moves from the persona's firm stand not to indulge in petty pursuits and romantic ideals, to a refusal to bow to the dictates of writing poetry according to the demands of the ex-coloniser's English literature. The personal confidence moves to the larger arena of national confidence in a land of plenty, but the use of the adverbial conjunction "And yet . .." and the question posed at the end is ominous in its restraint.

Ee is regarded as one of the few Malaysian poets who most consistently and successfully attempted to imbue local texture and colour by the use of idioms and colloquialisms. Ee himself said:

> The Malaysian writer worth his salt ought to be able to deal with everyday Malaysian [English] patios as it comes. The touchstone of his creativity and work would lie in the originality and insight, the necessity and inventiveness manifested in the text, and, in the final analysis, in his mastery of the language.

> (1988, p. 22)

The "inventiveness" with language is a feature of what is generally known as nativisation or domestication of the English language. It is a feature concurrent with the defining of indigenous or "native" themes in new literatures/postcolonial writing. The bilingual (or multilingual) writer "de-Englishes the language" through various linguistic processes, from the basic identifying of local artifacts, and phenomenon to the use of rhetorical strategies specific to the native culture (Kachru, 1987). Whatever the contextual and stylistic innovations, in whatever discourse, the processes are distinctly culture-bound. For Ee, his cultural landscape was a mix of native cultures, not one native culture.

By mixing linguistic and cultural variants of the environment he was in, Ee constantly reiterated his stance for a Malaysian pluralism, a sense of "multicultural influences working towards synthesis". Certainly there is no dearth of the artifacts and materials on Malaysian life: laterite, gong, *chichak*, soursops, sackcloth, latex, *padi*. At the slightly higher level are aspects and phenomenon of the Malaysian environment and landscape that are tapped for metaphors and symbolic effect: *fajar, pariah,* yam leaf, *tembusu* and *belukar*.

At a higher level still, the Malaysian sensibility is further captured by the bilingual poet's creativity in tapping the vast "verbal repertoire" of Malaysia's speech communities; for example, code-switching. Ee often uses local idioms in which the rhythms of Malaysian English of different speakers and rhythms of speech of different Malaysian languages are captured. In *Song of a Young Malaysian*, there is gentle humour in the ironic confessions of a young man who admits to be less than artistic, yet at the same time exudes a kind of confident bravado which successfully comes across in his laconic, disarming Malaysian English.

With Ee, there is the natural inclination towards certain stylistic devices and thematic emphasis internalised over the years, drawn from English and Western literature. Indeed Ee is a good example of the postcolonial writer as a hybridised entity who in his efforts to nativise the English language consistently integrates, or cross-fertilises (hybridises) the cultural signs and practices from the colonising and colonised cultures from old and new, from east and west, from one ethnic group and another. Chin WPH draws our attention to Ee's consistent use of "the classic weapons of irony" of Western literary tradition to emphasise alienation by highlighting marginalisation, abuse, corruption and injustice. (Chin, 1985). This aspect of Ee's style will be discussed later in his more mature poems when the integration of imported strategies and resources of his own (mixed) cultural heritage is consistently carried out:

> The writer in our time, in a time of crisis, must be free but alive, aware of the political dimension to his craft or vocation, of the potential role of language for constructive purposes.

(1988, p. 24)

In poems such as *Requiem*, *Arrival*, *The Times*, *The Morals*, *For My Son*, and *Justice and Patriotism*, the need to be truly "constructive" is seen in the more explicit, more politically-charged, communally-charged litany of hurts. The voice is more emphatic but the most memorable are those in which the frustration is tinged with sadness and regret.

Ee's later poems offer further examples of the use of local colour and idioms and/or strategies from Western literary tradition. *Mr. Tan Muses*, *Pengkalan Chepa*, *Kelantan* (from the book *Myths*), and *Tranquerah Road* and *Fire in Kampung Aman Sentosa* (from the book *Tranquerah*) fix the Malaysianness of place and people. Once again, nativisation often works hand in hand with Ee's use of the poetic tools of English literature; indirection, ellipsis, irony, humour, innuendo and allusion (Chin, 1985). This is especially so when outright criticism was dangerous and certain subjects forbidden. The use of various masks for the narrative voice/persona—the diffident spokesman, the ingénue, the tentative, ineffectual victim, the beaten man who almost gives up—allow Ee the use of irony, sarcasm, innuendo and understatement to place on record bitter grievances. Such examples occur in many of Ee's later poems but attention here will be focused on poems in *Myths*.

In the poem *Cycle*, indirection and innuendo are employed to portray an ominous sense of approaching danger. The sense of unremitting conflict, negotiation, cover-up and forebodings for the future are listed out to allude to possible betrayal, a large-scale impasse. However there is nothing specific about what "this" is, except its embodiment of profitless energy, of dislocation as felt by someone caught in the predictable as much as the unpredictable. The title itself is ambiguous. Will the final dislocation be deferred because of the cycle of events, or is there no end in sight to the cycle of anguish? In the same way, *Kuala Lumpur* ironically celebrates the big business of the building industry and by not mentioning the real builders of Kuala Lumpur (to Ee the ordinary man, or the labourers, specifically Chinese) Ee employs sarcasm and contrast for effect. The mindless worship of material progress and status, the ingratitude, the strutting, are the order of the day, carried out at the expense of "the common good" sarcastically described by the persona as "grand illusions".

In *Tranquerah*, even though distance allows detachment and straight talking in many of the poems, the use of understatement, of indirection and innuendo are still employed as may be seen in *Expectations, Disinherited* and *New Order*. The last two poems of *Myths: On Writing a Poem* and *Epilogue* look out to the shift in stance and tone of Ee's last two volumes. Both hint at the poet's leaving of the country: "a universe/on fire—and the final sacrifice"; and in the *Epilogue*, we read of the "mediator, at the crossroads", unable to keep " in tune with a newly—established sensibility". The *Epilogue* also sets the tone direct, no-holds-barred criticism (Karpal Singh, 1988). Yet, the emotional and aesthetic need to go back to the place he has left results in some of the best of Ee's poetry and convinces us that "to be simple is to involved/in a whole chaos, the claims and the counterclaims of mind, heart, word… "

Tranquerah, therefore, is a mix of the direct and angry, the sad and wistful, towards all that is distant and at the same time all that is internalised. In *New Order*, the façade of new nationalism and subsequent destruction of heritage is addressed. *Excursion* utilises the metaphor of journey (gone awry) to condemn the new progress. Sarcasm and bitter irony come into play in *Fire in Kampung Aman*

Sentosa, Disinherited, Certificate of Fitness, and poems of the May 13 riots and the aftermath. *Exile, Departure* and *Musing on a Departure* trace facets of pain and inevitability of exile. The immediacy of feelings, ranging from disillusionment, despondency, humiliation, regret and anger contrast with the distanced objectivity of *Kuala Lumpur, May 1969, New Year Eve, Jalan Kilang, Malaysian Friendship* and *Epilogue.* In the long poem in *Tranquerah Road,* from which the collection takes its name, Ee returns to the old haunts as he records the story of his personal anguish: from multicultural idealism to self-exile against frames of multicultural, multifaceted happenings in Tranquerah Road, in Malacca, and ultimately in the country; where finally, all is not as it should be where "our mangled heritage" is all that is left of "the earth and sea and sky / and rainbow, golden dream…"

1.3   Conclusion

The sheer volume of Ee's poems is held together by the personality and convictions of the man. To think of Ee's work is to remember the poet's spare style, without embellishments, the free verse that effectively captures the speaking voice, the moral tone, the sue to local colours and domestication of English, and the easy drawing of resources from the wide store of styles, allusions and images of foreign traditions. But to think of Ee is also to think immediately of the thematic concerns connected with alienation. His poems record the dislocation of a member of the Baba community, of the Chinese community, at the workplace amongst the covetous and self-seeking, within the larger Malaysian community. Even the literary community at home and abroad (especially in relation to his use of the English language), and the controversial matters he raised. It would be so easy to regard Ee as the producer of angry, ironic, sarcastic poems in which he railed, relentlessly against bureaucracy, moral corruption, monoculturalism, double speak and treachery, racial animosity and, racial and personal victimisation. We should also consider those poems which afford insights into the refined, widely read, deeply sensitive man and poet who saw his work in terms of helping to build a humane, cooperative society. Thus, we should remember the nostalgia and sadness over the loss of a quieter yet richer past, in poems like *Tranquerah Road* and *Heeran Street*, and the strong presence of Malacca in some of the poems in *Nearing a Horizon*. There are also the heartfelt tributes to the natural beauties of Malaysia. *On a Suggestion that I Make a Song About You* (*Myths*) is a moving record of the poet's love for the country. Yet it would be particularly important for readers and writers now, and it would be something Ee would have liked, to see poems such as *Kuala Lumpur* (*I of the Many Faces*) and *For My Son* (*Myths*) as lessons and reminders for the critical times we live in. Thus, Ee Tiang Hong's poems provide a moving record of a man caught in specific circumstances he could not and would not accept. What comes across is a body of work that is sensitive, committed, relevant and durable, not "stiff" and "stark" but versatile and steadfast as his *Tembusu*.

Bibliography

Primary Texts

Ee, Tiang Hong. (1960). *I of the many faces*. Malacca: Wah Seong Press Ltd.

———. (1973). *Lines written in Hawaii*. Hawaii: East West Centre.

———. (1976). *Myths for a wilderness*. Singapore: Heinemann Asia Ltd.

———. (1991). *Nearing a horizon*. Singapore: Unipress.

———. (1988). Literature and liberation: the price of freedom. In E. Thumboo (ed.), *Literature and liberation* (pp. 11–41). Manila: Solidaridad Publications.

———. (1987). History as a myth in Malaysian poetry in English. In K. Singh (ed.), *The writer's sense of the past*. (pp.10–16). Singapore: Singapore University Press.

Secondary Texts

Chin, W. P. H. (1985). Hybrid blooms: The emergent poetry in English of Malaysia and Singapore. In C. Koelb & S. Noakes (ed.), *The comparative perspective on literature* (pp. 130-146). Ithaca, New York: Cornell University Press.

Haskell, D. (1996). Cultural crosses: Ee Tiang Hong's *Nearing a horizon*. In B. Bennett et al. (eds.), *Crossing cultures* (pp. 133–140). London: Skoob Books.

Kachru, B. (1987). The bilingual's creativity: Discoursal and stylistic strategies in contact literatures. In L. Smith (ed.), *Discourse across cultures*. (pp. 125-141). New York: Prentice Hall

Lim, S. G. (1994). *Writing Southeast Asia in English: Against the grain*. London: Skoob Books.

Maniam, K. S. & Shanmughalingham, M. (Comps). (1988). *An anthology of Malaysian poetry*. Kuala Lumpur. Dewan Bahasa dan Pustaka.

O'Sullivan, V. (1986). The poetry of Ee Tiang Hong. *CRNLE Reviews Journal*, (1), (pp. 1–15.)

Singh, K. (1988). The only way out: Sense of exile in the poetry of Ee Tiang Hong. In M. A. Quayum & P. Wicks (Eds.), *Malaysian literature in English: A critical reader 2001* (226–233). Malaysia: Longman.

Thumboo, E. (1973). *Seven poets*. Singapore: Singapore University Press.

Thumboo, E. (1976). *The second tongue: An anthology of poetry from Malaysia and Singapore*. Singapore: Heinemann Educational Books (Asia) Ltd.

Notes

1.   There are references to the first collection having "appeared" in 1956 and there is every possibility that the poems were published in the year before Malaysia gained its independence. The 1960 date for this chapter is based on the text available, first published in 1960 by Wah Seong Press in Jonker Street, Malacca.

2.   Ee's poems in his second volume *Lines Written in Hawaii* have not been included in the discussions. These are poems and verse of a personal nature considered of lesser relevance to the focus of this volume. For the same reason, many of the poems in *Nearing a Horizon* have not been dealt with in detail.

3.   These are examples from *I of the Many Faces*. There are many other examples from other collections.

Edward Dorall

2.0 Epigraph

…I have attempted to reproduce the fragmentary speech which can be heard throughout Malaysia. Drama, I feel, should be truthful, and any dialogue which does not utilise the actual rhythms and mannerisms of the people can only be unrealistic, therefore false…

— Edward Dorall
"Note on the Dialogue"
for *A Tiger is Loose in Our Community*

2.1 Introduction

Dorall was born in 1936 in Kuala Lumpur and went to school in Malaysia, India and the United Kingdom. He graduated from Trinity College in 1958 with a degree in Modern Languages. He taught English in Paris for two years; French in Guernsey, Channel Islands for a year then taught English at the Victoria Institution for four years. In 1970, he was awarded his M. A. for his research and thesis on Sean O'Casey.

In 1967, he was appointed lecturer in the English Department of the University of Malaya. Dorall is now with the New Straits Times. He has a weekly section, "Classical Briefing", in which he reviews classical music in its various forms of production. Dorall occasionally reviews texts of a literary nature. In 1993, he was one of three judges (with Wong Phui Nam and Salleh Joned) on the panel for the *NST*-Shell Poetry Competition.

Edward Dorall is an important pioneer figure in Malaysian drama in English. In the 1960s and 1970s, Dorall, with dramatists such as Lee Joo Hor and Patrick Yeoh were leading figures in the Malaysian endeavour to establish a Malaysian presence in drama activities. More specifically their plays in English, about Malaysians, concerned with Malaysian issues and contexts were vibrant, workable contributions to the overall efforts by individuals and groups to develop a Malaysian theatre in Malay or English but written, produced, managed and acted by Malaysians (Fernando, 1971).

Dorall's plays explore issues connected with the socio-political context of early Malaysia and the situation of the individual in it. Against the dynamic yet volatile multicultural milieu, the gulf between have and have-nots and the powers of state ideology, Dorall's protagonists wrestle with themselves, with victimisation and with maintaining some kind of virtue and integrity in these conditions. The general, and sometimes abstract portrayal of the condition of poverty, missed opportunities, victimisation will later concretise in the more specific, detailed studies of alienation and "unhomeliness" in subsequent poetry and much of the fiction of Malaysian literature in English.

It is in the early plays that nativisation of English began its dynamic contribution as an integral part of Malaysian writing in English. Dorall's plays provide rich examples of the immediacy and effectiveness of Malaysian English in detailing the specificities of place, people and time in Malaysian creative writing. Although Dorall's last play *The Death of the Old Man* was written in 1993, his continued involvement in the literary scene of Malaysia, especially in his reviews of literary texts, serves to remind us of his deep-rooted connection with Malaysian literature and with the use of English in the many senses of the word, in the country.

2.2   Discussion of works:
The following is a list of Dorall's plays with the year of production given where available. Apart from *A Tiger Is Loose in Our Community* (henceforth referred to *Tiger*) and *The Hour of the Dog*, as far as the writers of this book are aware of, all other texts have not been published in book form.

*   *Arise O Youth!* (Produced in 1966)

- *The Young Must be Strong* (Produced in 1967)
- *A Tiger Is Loose in Our Community* (Produced in 1967)
- *A Time for a Man to Say No* (No dates available)
- *The Hour of the Dog* (Produced in 1970)
- *The Foolishness of God* (Produced in 1971)
- *The Death of the Old Man* (No dates available)

The Death of the Old Man won the third prize in the 1993 *NST*-Esso Playwriting Competition. It is the last part of a trilogy that began with *The Hour of the Dog* and *The Foolishness of God*.

Dorall's reviews of literary texts that have appeared in literary books and in the *New Straits Times* "Literary" sections include those of the *Skoob Pacifica Anthologies 1* and *2* (in 1993 and 1994 respectively); of Chuah Guat Eng's *Echoes of Silence* (1994); of K. S. Maniam's *The Return* (1993) and of Wong Phui Nam's poetry (2001).

As producer in both senses of writing and seeing through many of his plays for public performance, Dorall's status in the development of Malaysian theatre and Malaysian writing is undeniable. His plays are socially-committed texts aimed at raising awareness of the social and political problems of a young country in the throes of nation building and modernisation. For his plays, Dorall drew on new materials at hand: his own Eurasian background and experiences, his exposure to languages and the manners and mannerisms of different languages; his experience with English language teaching; the world of young people, classroom and school, his training and expertise in English literature, drama and music.

Edward Dorall's contribution to Malaysian drama in English requires a brief mention of the context of Malaysian theatre in the 1950s and early 1960s. In the postwar years and with the re-occupation of Malaya and Singapore by the British, theatre in the country was dominated by the colonials. Although a group called the Malaysian Arts Theatre Group (MATG) attempted to correct the imbalance, little actual progress was made to address the non-existence of Malaysian producers, playwrights and stage people until the 1960s. The only Malaysian theatre written, produced and arranged and acted by Malaysians was confined to the Malay drama and the plays of writers such as Kala Dewata, A. Samad Said and Usman Awang. Those involved in theatre in English, which were divorced from the new energies of drama in Malay, had to rise above the compartmentalisation brought about by language issues. They had to initiate the process of independence, first with all-Malaysian casts, then with new Malaysian plays.

This was the general scenario when Edward Dorall, a teacher of English, caught public attention. He won the Arts Council Playwriting Competition (1965) with his play *The Young Must Be Strong*. In the following year his second play *Arise O Youth!* was the first Malaysian play in English to be given a public performance. In March 1967, *Tiger* had its first performance; this was followed a few months later with his first play being staged in Kuantan. According to Fernando:

> Dorall must be given credit for being first in the field
> in both writing and producing Malaysian plays in English
> which enjoyed popular success.

> (1972, p. ix)

By the end of 1970, there were more than twenty-five Malaysian plays written in English (Fernando: ix). Fernando's collection of six plays in *New Drama One* (1972), and *New Drama Two* (1972) includes two of Dorall's plays. Apart from indicating Dorall's productivity and involvement in Malaysian theatre, the plays' thematic concerns exemplify major concerns of Malaysian literature in English, which will crop up again and again in the works of other writers and in other genres.

It is to these two plays published in the collections Fernando edited that we now turn to discuss features of context and style. *Tiger* is set mainly in a squatter settlement on the outskirts of Kuala Lumpur. The protagonists are young boys caught in the vicious grip of poverty, irresponsible uncaring adults, prejudice of class divisions and the rules of survival that require and allow violence and aggression to take place. Chan Choon Hoong (Tiger), his sister Helen and younger brother San Fan are all denied the opportunity to leave the squalor of their lives. Kaliappan, the simpleton is used by weak yet dangerous elements to kill Tiger. Although minor characters, the lethal combination of Pillai, Hashim, Siew and Low suggest the potential danger and uncertainties faced by a community at the hands of opportunists and rebel-rousers.

Poverty, class inequality and class struggles are the social and economic ills Dorall chooses to emphasise. There is racial prejudice that contributes to Philip Reade and Helen Chan going their separate ways but at a time when the rhetoric of racial inequality would have been present in the country (late 1960s), the play chooses to foreground class inequalities and the destructive anarchic effects of poverty. The neglect and propensity for violence that the "masses" share cut across racial divisions. Dorall's social concerns are similar to those we see in works of writers active in the 1960s and 1970s: Ee Tiang Hong in his poems; Ghulam Sarwar Yousof in his play *Halfway Road, Perang* (1982); and in the collection of short stories edited by Lloyd Fernando (1968 and 1981).

Anthony Price (1974) reviewed *Arise O Youth!* and *A Time for a Man to Say No* (Price 1974:3). Commenting on the nativisation of English, Price quotes from Dorall's Preface to *Arise O Youth!* in which he says that he has given his characters:

A selection of the language which people in their social class would actually use. The problem that arises is whether the resulting pidgin English, with tenses limited, or absent altogether, pronouns confused, plurals often ignored, vocabulary unadventurous, and the whole punctuated by "ah's," "lah's" and "wah's"—the problem is whether this crippled but colourful dialect can be used extensively in drama, not only for comic and realistic effect, but also for pathos and tragedy.

(1974, p. 4)

Dorall's ability with comic dialogue is praised, and with regard to Dorall's own reservations about Malysian English and tragedy, Price also concludes that the language Dorall gives to his characters is not only "convincingly Malaysian" but also "supple enough to be used for all the moods and styles required by drama". Attention is drawn to the fact that Dorall carefully distinguishes between the speech of characters of different races and of different social classes, age and sex.

Fernando's comments are more guarded. He sees Dorall's "concentrated Malaysianisms" as creating problems relating to character portrayal and dramatic impact. For Fernando, Dorall's Malaysian English plays "run away with him" (1972, p. xii). As will be noted from the quote given earlier, Dorall himself was not unaware of the potential shortcomings of using Malaysian English. In his note on the Dialogue, which gives instructions to the actors of *Tiger*, he reiterates this:

> The great disadvantage of fragmentary speech . . . is that while it lends itself to comic situations it is not ideally suited to serious moods.
>
> (Cited in Fernando, 1972, p.2)

In spite of all this, Dorall's earlier plays will be remembered for the adept and generally successful nativisation of English particularly in highlighting the vibrancy of his young protagonists, and to reinforce linguistic variations brought about by economic and social status, ethnic grouping, sex and age. The example given below shows Dorall's ability to capture the nuances of differing values, outlook and intentions of his characters. Philip, from a middle class Eurasian family has brought his friends to the house and they meet his parents for the first time. Mr. Reade considers the likes of Helen and her brother Choon Hoong (Tiger) as "riff-raff of society":

Philip [embarrassed] : Oh, Dad, this is Choon Hoong… and this is Helen.

Mr. Reade : Hullo. [he calls out] Amah!

Philip	:	Helen, my father and mother.
Mrs. Reade	:	Philip has told us a lot about you.
Helen	:	I'm—very happy to meet you.
Mr. Reade	:	Amah!

Amah (entering, trying to show to the visitors that she can hold her own with her employers)

Amah:	:	What?
Mr. Reade	:	Here! (dumping parcels onto the table) Take inside. And orange juice fall down. Get cloth and wipe ah?
Tiger	:	That's all right, I can do it.
Mr. Reade	:	It's not necessary. Amah will do it.
Amah	:	Tcha! I tole Philip she no careful she blake glass.

(*Tiger*, pp. 52–53)

Another interesting aspect in *A Tiger Is Loose in the Community* is the use of songs and music. The Tiger theme song is confident and strident at the beginning of the play, ironic at the close. Then there is Kali's bird song (Act 1, Scene II). Specific instructions as to the way the theme song should be sung indicate Dorall's attempt to highlight the divisions in society and potential dangers ahead for the community. Although Choon Hoong the Tiger is dead, as somberly acknowledged in the closing theme song, another tiger, his brother, takes his place. At a more ironic level, another ferocious danger in the form of prejudice, hatred and violence is set free in the community. The effect at the end of the play, of the racially mixed rebel-rousers—Siew, Low, Hashim, Pillai—coming together only in violence to use the innocent scapegoat Kali and get even with Tiger, is unsettling and ominous.

The play foregrounds social problems existing in new Malaysia and in doing so highlights future unrest and dislocation with rifts and conflicts arising from modernisation and lack of meaningful integration at various levels. At the same time, in the plight of its young protagonists, misunderstood and marginalised yet full of energy and the potential for good, it bears testimony to Dorall's close interaction with young people, with music and with English. Of the play, Fernando writes:

> The whole play is undeniably a work of love, an excellent vehicle for schools' production, disarmingly navïe in conception . . . consistent in execution.
>
> (1972, p. xiii)

The Hour of the Dog is a departure from the earlier play. Apart from the absence of songs or music, the chronological sequence of events of one week in the earlier play gives way to a "here and now" setting with the stage divided into sections with simultaneous and connected episodes going on to suggest one man's conflict within himself and with outside forces. The scenes of the play are cleverly and dramatically constructed to be "facets of an invisible whole". Nicks One to Four are different "selves" of the protagonist Nick who lies in bed wrestling with his own conscience even as he wrestles with his interrogators. Facets of his personality are erected as the various Nicks argue, abuse, relent and capitulate to authoritarian figures. Nick's surrender to the larger, stronger forces of authoritarian power highlights his alienation and ineffectual attempts at personal liberty.

If one may see a range of features that mark the various influences and motivation behind the postcolonial writer, including the nativisation of the language in *Tiger*, the *Hour of the Dog* provides additional features as to the varied nature of the schema and influences the postcolonial writer brings to his works. There are important allusions drawn from Christianity which, whilst they do not mar appreciation of the play as a whole to the uninitiated, provide pleasure and insight when their relevance is understood. The epigraph from Peter, with its reminder of lapsed righteousness, acts as a counterpoint to the Impersonator's Christian allusions used to dismantle Nick's faith in himself. In its implicitly absurdist, post-modernist presentation of an individual wrestling with himself and privy to the other interactions going on between the protagonists' other selves and forces of authority, *The Hour of the Dog* marks a development in Dorall's creativity. Yet both plays are sombre, dark portrayals of lost initiative in barren, inhospitable environments.

In a discussion on early Malaysian playwrights, *An Exploded Consciousness: Towards a definition of history in selected plays of Lee, Yeoh, Dorall and Das*, Margaret Yong writes of the "historical trauma" exposed in varying degrees and styles in the pioneering works of these writers. Despite differences in presentation there is "inner cohesion" in these works. The plays portray the blankness of history; there is no stable sense of the past to illuminate, to "be understood as an identifiable and identifying continuous tradition of collective existence, which the individual may draw upon" (1986, p. 23).

In *Tiger*, there is violence with no resolution from or into the past; a world of violent action rules. In *The Hour of the Dog* memory of the past is not to be trusted, in fact it becomes an "act of will" as all the Nicks are figments of the puppeteer Nick's imagination, manipulated to re-create the past. In the end the creations possess him and Dorall's final stage directions seal Nick's self-destructive end in the anarchical present.

2.3   Conclusion

Dorall's plays, as those by the early playwrights of the 1960s and 1970s, are significant creative products of the writers' desire for involvement in the early, unsteady steps towards nationhood, creative writing and theatre. In foregrounding class inequalities and poverty, community chaos and violence, Dorall's plays are significant milestones in the development of Malaysian literature generally and more significantly of Malaysian theatre, especially political theater in the country. Today, the plays of Kee Thuan Chye and Huzir Sulaiman address cultural and political issues specific to the times in Malaysian English as vibrant and natural as the dialogue in Dorall's plays.

In a review of *Southeast Asia Writes Back! Skoob Pacifica Anthology No. 1* (1993), and with reference to the collection of works from Singapore, Dorall writes:

> The Singaporeans . . . are all truthful and accomplished, and also clinically cold. Here again when will people learn that the greatest art is positive? Only to tell the nasty truth is only to diagnose a disease—very necessary, we are grateful for such honesty and all that—but we remember best what uplifts us, what we can share in.

(1994, p. 32)

An aspect of this attitude is seen in the reviews Dorall writes. He always emphasises what is positive and best in the texts under scrutiny. In his plays however, Dorall is different. Certainly in the two plays discussed here there is a sense of uncertainty and of menace as the "good" people struggle to get some kind of a foothold in an unkind unsafe world.

Bibliography

Primary Texts

Dorall, E. (1972). A tiger is loose in our community. In L.Fernando (ed.), *New drama one* (pp. 1–82). Kuala Lumpur: Oxford University Press.

———. (1972). The hour of the dog. In L. Fernando (ed.), *New drama two* (pp. 17–149). Kuala Lumpur: Oxford University Press.

———. (1993, December 1). Rojak mix out of geographical mix-up. (Review of the book *Southeast Asia Writes Back! Skoob Pacifica anthology No.1*). *New Straits Times*, (p. 32.)

———. (1994, September 28). An orgy of sin and semen. (Review of the book *The pen is mightier than the sword: Skoob Pacifica anthology No. 2*). *New Straits Times*, (p. 31.)

Wong, P. N. (2001). Against the wilderness. (Review of the book *Against the Wilderness*). *Tenggara, 43*, (pp.148–152.)

Secondary Texts

Fernando, L. (ed.). (1972). *Introduction: New drama one.* Kuala Lumpur: Oxford University Press.

Price, A. (1974). This crippled, colourful dialect: The language of Malaysian plays. *Journal of Commonwealth Literature, IX*(1), (pp.3–10.)

Yong, M. (1986). An exploded consciousness: Toward a definition of history in selected plays of Lee, Yeoh, Dorall and Das. *ACLALS Bulletin, 7*(3), (pp.19–25.)

Wong Phui Nam

3.0 Epigraph

Where we ourselves to-day is a wilderness. It is a wilderness for its origins in serving the imperatives of commodity markets. It has, as one of the consequences, possessed the word only imperfectly. As a sign that has abstracted itself from the sensuous body and inwardness of the world, the word here works almost wholly to define such useful concerns as exchange, property, hierarchies, technologies—even desires and wants. We have let it simplify us collectively into a factor of production, into consumers and a few among us, owners as well, of the wherewithal to produce, and helped it neutralise the distinction between the empowered and marginalised... As with any utterance in the wilderness, there is in the mere need for making these poems, an implicit faith in the existence of a moral order appearances to the contrary in these unpromising times.

—Wong Phui Nam, *Against the Wilderness*
(2000, p. i)

3.1 Introduction

Wong Phui Nam was born on September 20, 1935 in Kuala Lumpur. He is the seventh child in the family. His mother who was from China passed away when he was only three years old, while his father who was from Malacca passed away when Wong Phui Nam was nine years old. Since then, Wong Phui Nam and his siblings were looked after by his "amah" (servant cum nanny) who was also from China.

Wong Phui Nam received his early education at the Batu Road School in the morning, while in the afternoon, he attended a

Confucian Chinese school. He received secondary education at the Victoria Institution. Even while in secondary school Wong continued attending Chinese language and literature classes in the afternoons. He graduated from the University of Malaya (then in Singapore) with a degree in Economics and has since worked mainly in development finance and merchant banking. Wong has worked with several financial institutions including Pesaka Capital, a company dealing with finance and insurance; Standard Chartered Bank, The Ministry of Commerce and Industry, Bangkok Bank (in Thailand) and the Malaysian Industrial Development Finance (MIDF).

While at college, he was actively involved in *The New Cauldron*, the student magazine of Raffles College. The college later became the University of Malaya. He was also co-editor of *Litmus One*, an anthology of university verse.

Wong Phui Nam is among the few Malaysians who write poetry in English. Most of Wong Phui Nam's poetry written in the 1960s first appeared in an anthology of Malaysian writings entitled *Bunga Emas* published in the United Kingdom in 1963. They were subsequently compiled and published as *How the Hills Are Distant* in 1966 (a *Tenggara* supplement) by the Department of English, University of Malaya. During much of the 1970s and 1980s, Wong Phui Nam did not publish any new works. In 1989, he published his second volume of poetry called *Remembering Grandma and Other Rumours*. This volume was published by the Department of English, National University of Singapore. Wong's poetry has also been published in *Seven Poets*, *The Second Tongue*, *The Flowering Tree*, *Young Commonwealth Poets*, *Tenggara*, *Temasek*, *Collections of Poems from India, Sri Lanka, Singapore and Malaya, Southeast Asian Review of English*, *Westerley* and *Sare*.

Wong Phui Nam married Khatijah bt Ismail in 1968, and took the name Mohammed Razali. The couple have four children, Sharin, Nor Azah, Rizal and Qushairi.

During his free time, he enjoys reading the works of other literary writers from around the world. Some of his favourite authors and poets are Judith Wright, Hart Craine, Rimbaud, Baudelaire, Tu Fu, Li Bai and T'ao Yuan Ming. Wong Phui Nam is also renowned in Malaysia as a discerning literary critic, especially on poetry in various languages such as English, Mandarin and Bahasa Malaysia. He also used to write a fortnightly literary column in the *New Straits Times* called "Other Cadences" on the works of authors from various countries.

Wong Phui Nam is the most important and most prolific Malaysian writing poetry in English. His works are distinctly marked by the depth of their involvement in the psyche of the Malaysian Chinese community. To be able to understand the major concerns of Wong Phui Nam's writings, it is first necessary to understand what he calls as "Malaysian condition":

It is a condition (admittedly seen from a personal perspective, that of the Chinese immigrant community) of being bereft of any memory longer than a personal and family one, neither of which, by its nature, goes very far into the past. It is a condition of not knowing any tradition which has survived to the present from long ages past living masters in the arts and in spiritual wisdom, and of not being able to refer back to a text or an artifact and say that this is the creation of a direct antecedent and so, a source of life that sustains what I do now as a writer. It is a condition of absence of other than a debased form of belief, not through loss but through not having inherited even a minor tradition to begin with, and one which lacks cohesion in the communal life for its being called into existence in the first place by the dictates of thorough-going exploitation of resources to serve modern capitalist markets. In sum, it is mere subsistence and, as I have written elsewhere, subsistence as an orphaned psyche.

(Wong, 1995 p.33)

Wong Phui Nam's poetry is both historical and psychological at one time. It is historical in that it charts through the experiences of mainly the Malaysian Chinese community, their arrival, "progress" and development in this country. His works transverse the ancient and the legendary through to actual histories of arrival and struggle to the dilemmas that inhabit the post-modern Malaysian mind. Psychologically, they invade the painful memories etched in personal and social history in deliberation of issues such identity, culture, sense of belonging, alienation and challenges of nationhood.

Wong Phui Nam's poetry are significant in that they signpost the birth and development of a multiracial and multicultural Malaysia. The signs in his poetry are ones that awaken Malaysian sensibilities to the problems of the Chinese "Other", often seen as resilient, and affected by the tribulations of this emerging postcolonial multiracial nation.

3.2 Discussion of works

In most of Wong Phui Nam's works, his concerns about cultural deprivation, "psychic nakedness" and Malaysia as a "wasteland" can be found. Therefore, very much influenced by his concerns, the themes of his poems include cultural loss, loss of identity, exile, disorientation, disorder or internal conflict, alienation and death. His tones and themes draw his audience into the mind of the poet where they find desolation, desperation and despair. Wong Phui Nam's consistent use of the personal voice reflects an attempt to weld himself to the experiences dramatised in his poetry.

The foundation of Wong Phui Nam's poetry rests on the multi-ethnic Malaysian, socio-cultural and political environment, and its minefield of tension and sensitivities. Centuries of living together has taught the Malaysian people the skills of tolerance, tact and artful accommodation, while driving underground interracial ailments such as prejudice, fear and lack of understanding.

The poems suggest that a sense of uneasiness remains beneath the appearance of racial harmony. Wong's poetry delves into the core of this uneasiness resulting in states of confusion and disillusionment that stem from individual and societal attempts to make sense of an uncertain place called "home".

Wong is very much influenced by the Muse and his own experience. On the Muse, he wrote " . . . on every occasion of writing a poem, the poet: is in effect invoking her presence, which becomes manifest in the persona that inhabits and 'speaks' the poem" (1995, p. 24).

According to Wong, writing poetry must come from within oneself. It is often about something one knows well and not about something alien. He views life both as the teacher and source of ideas. It is only through experiences that one gets ideas and inspirations of what life really is and about kinds of people one may encounter in the journey of life. In other words, it's through experiences that one may apprehend the world; by emotions, intellect, intuition and physical sensation. Poetry conveys all these simultaneously—it is then a unified perception of the world. He states that "All forms of art is like a dream, finding a public expression in a realm of words if you're a writer, in a realm of sound if you're a musician, in a realm of colours, shapes and forms if you're a painter" (1995, p.25).

Wong's earlier works published in the collection, *How the Hills Are Distant*, contain recurrent themes of exile, loss of identity and a yearning for an idealised past (Thumboo, 1976). The epic poem, *How the Hills Are Distant* portrays a struggle to carve a place of one's own within a new environment. The poem reflects the problems faced by a minority group, originally immigrant, at coming to terms with the adopted land. Though the poem can be viewed from a racial-cultural position, it also depicts a personal struggle in search of identity. For the minority and immigrant individual, the struggle to shape and reshape his identity is continuous because society and its social, cultural and political structures are changing constantly.

The poem seems to allude to the immigrant's need and attempt to adapt, first under the British rule and then under "self-rule" as a demanding one. The predicament seems magnified especially when self-rule does not allow for complete racial, cultural and individual autonomy hence necessitating the need to accommodate and be tolerated within a minority-majority socio-political structure. Each change requires the individual to prove his loyalty; yet the line between loyalty and subservience is at best blurred. The frustration of non-acceptance and the continuous need to prove oneself seems to create a traumatic identity crisis. The individual faces the reality that the hope for a new identity is an uncertain one, possible maybe, only with the loss of the existing one. The persona depicts this vividly and with the smell of death as "imminent" amidst the "wet grass" and the "frangipani":

> ...against the margin of encroaching
> sleep when I anticipate only, a waking to
> vague rememberence of a harrowing in my
> dream

(1968, p. 2)

It seems apparent that the loss of his identity is nightmarish. The title of the collection, *How the Hills Are Distant* seems to convey the difficulty of arriving at a decision of giving up an existing identity, and of attaining the elusive new one. Wong (as cited in Thumboo, 1976) has said of *How the Hills Are Distant*:

> These poems need to be written. They are of a time, of a place, of a people who find themselves to live by institutions and folk ways which are not their own, having to absorb the manners of language not their own.

(1976, p. 7)

Wong's poems hint at conditions where even in self rule the minority other is branded "immigrant" by the exclusive stamp of national identity. This seems to lead the persona into a state of self-exile, not wanting to let go of his culture and traditions, a way of life with which he is secure. The situation is further exacerbated when attempts to integrate and readiness to be assimilated are rewarded with suspicion and resistance.

Poem for a Birthday depicts the persona's inability to identify with the land and his "external identity," that which is assigned to him by society:

> To be most myself is to be
> this darkness that pervades the land.

(1988, p. 18)

"This darkness that pervades" is the darkness he feels within and without. It seems that the migrant minority is has to live two lives. His true self in private and another self in public. That which he is essentially, then, is regarded as threatening and undesirable. Hence to him, that desolate and isolated state is reality. The ironic contrast between the title and the sombre tone of the poem renders stark the bleakness of "birth", the creation of a new identity that is meaningless to the persona. "Authentic" identity and essential self are reflected as "the darkness that pervades the land", implying that identity cannot be synthetically created and is not always what is visible. The propagation of a synthetic national identity by cultural alchemists leads to the suppression of true identity wrought from natural processes ingrained within culture and tradition. Wong's poem demonstrates that the conflict between keeping the self intact while at the same time being an accepted member of a multiracial society results in a duality of identity, one authentic and hidden, the other superficial and apparent.

In *Nocturnes and Bagatelles*, Wong evokes feelings of alienation and loneliness. The persona laments in a solitude which is both physical with the passing of loved ones and psychological, through imposed and self-inflicted alienation. Desperate and desolate, the persona seems to appeal for acceptance not as a clone of society but for what he really is. He longs for a time when he can be himself and yet be part of society, for a time of complete and unconditional acceptance:

> How long must I bend
> In this uncertainty
> I in my thoughts like flowers
> to words every uncertain light.

(1968, p. 27)

Wong's second collection of poems, *Remembering Grandma and Other Rumours* deals with issues that concern the human condition in a changing world. There is an ironic rendition of a world that is moving forward with material progress leaving behind humanity in an "aspiritual" existence. *A Night Easter* and *Lazarus Recumbent*, though using Christian allusions ironically portray sentiments opposed to Christian tenets: faith, hope and charity become faithlessness, hopelessness and meanness. Easter is the celebration of the resurrection of Christ, triumph of life over death, but the poem ends in gloom and despair. The persona says:

> I cannot figure who there is
> who will move this boulder, this heavy
> fleshiness from the heart—

(1993, p. 122)

Wong uses religious and sensual imagery to convey a state of emotional and physical imprisonment. *Words for Easter* ends with a search for a miracle equal to the resurrection of Christ; it is a wish for what seems impossible. In *Lazarus Recumbent*, we see Lazarus reluctant to return to the world for fear of being alienated and victimised. In re-fashioning the story of Lazarus in this way, the poet echoes his feelings of disillusionment with and estrangement from his world, which has become barren of justice and morality. Lazarus reveals these sentiments as he contemplates returning to the world.

The poet mocks humanity's religious hypocrisy in *Out of the Desert*, discounting wrong doings in the name of God:

> You think it right that with claw and
> savage tooth you tear into entrails,
> break bones for marrow of all those
> among the living who must lay themselves
> upon the altar your god had you raise
> to yourself.

(1989, p. 42)

The attack on humanity is directed at the misuse and abuse of religion for self-serving, self-satisfying and deceitful purposes. The so-called "keepers" of religious faith sacrifice people at the altar that "their god" had them erect not to God but to themselves to satisfy their own religious egos. Many religions claim that man is made in the image of God. Ironically, the "keepers" of these faiths fail to realise that if they are unjust and cruel to any human being or groups of human beings, so must be their "god".

The examination of humanity and self continues in *The Caves* which takes the reader on a quest through the persona's mind in search of the core of self. What is visible is not pleasant. The "caves", representing a mindscape, are frightening, dark and gloomy. In addition, the search for the persona's identity within the mindscape is tortuous.

Wong's poems are not without their political undertones. In depicting the human condition, there are allusions to the problems of human co-existence in multiracial societies such as Malaysia. In a multiracial society, trust, understanding and justice are essential for peaceful and satisfactory co-existence. If the foundation of nationhood is suspect, then suspicion, distrust and fear will paralyse the nation. It is within such a context that "rumours" thrive best. Indications that Wong's rumours are based on truth are found in the prologue of this book: "As is the way with rumour, much of what is told here is smoke, but once—here and everywhere—there had been a fire." In this sense, these "rumours" are antithetical in that they are truths. His rumours are those of death, disease and decay. The "rumours" attempt to create awareness not only of the diseases of society but those of individuals. The ailments that kill in the poems, *Remembering Grandma, Fat Uncle Dying, Last Days in Hospital, Stepmother, Cousin* and *For My Old Amah,* are all cancerous diseases that work from within, unknown and unseen, until it is too late. It seems almost obvious that Wong is making a direct reference between the diseases of individuals and the amoral diseases that plague societies, nations and humanity.

Ways of Exile is a collection of previously published poems (in the 1960s and 1980s) with some new ones. The collection has four sections; *How the Hills Are Distant, For a Local Osiris, What Are the Roots...* and *Rumours of Exits.* In the preface to this collection Wong highlights the dilemma and problems of writing Malaysian poetry in English "out of stony rubbish". Appreciating this thought leads readers to a better understanding of his poetry and poetic aims. He describes modern Malaysia as an "enclave" where "greed, anger, lust, and a boastful pride of life are ...given free rein" amidst which there is a need to locate ways to remain attached to the human spirit. Wong is convinced that authenticity in the individual can only be achieved when the individual submits "himself to disciplines and be guided by the beliefs of the great religions". In his endeavour "to avoid inauthencity", Wong gives "primacy to immediate experience, to transform it into internal an event that assumes a sensory and emotional life of its own and then lets it find outward expression through the mediation of words which are organised as to give at the same time pointers to the possible meanings of the appropriated experience". Such an admission adds to the bleakness of messages in Wong's poetry in that they become intimately attached to reality, especially since the reality is a Malaysian one.

Essentially, this collection of poems does not move away from images of disillusionment and desperation, though one senses that the messages they convey have diverged from racial and sectional tones. *Address from the God* usurps the location and characteristics of the annual birth and death of a God of temperate climates, placing him in the strange and alienating locale of the tropics. Metamorphosed into a tropical God, Osiris remains in an endless state of death. The death of Osiris leaves humankind unprotected as demonstrated by the overpowering of human habitat, "the strangling buildings and subverting of all structural foundations". Osiris' death leaves the world in sickness and desolation. Wong's poem suggests that modernity does not always bring positive outcomes and even if in this situation Osiris was to rise, there is no guarantee that He would be recognised by humankind, making resurrection futile.

In Wong's re-reading of the poem *A Version from T'ao Yuan-Ming* in the section *What are the Roots…*, we witness an attempt to reshape cultural experiences. While the original poet's theme focuses on the withdrawal from the world, Wong re-reads the texts by placing it within present contexts, evolving from it disgust for bureaucracy and its unpredictable ways.

In the section *Rumours of Exits*, (which includes the poems *A Death in the Ward*, *A Night Easter*, *Temple Caves* and *From Chairil Anwar*) the exits in his poems do not represent escape or flight. On contrary, they divulge a sense of moving on from constraining ideas, thoughts and attitudes towards the widening of perspectives and recreation of personality. However, in Wong's own way, the notion of rumours become equated with truth and these "rumoured truth" are aimed at creating awareness of diseases that fester in societies and individuals. *A Death in the Ward* emphasises this thought by highlighting the human preoccupation with things to do with the flesh and its desires only to realise upon death that the questions and concerns that really matter remain unaddressed. *In Night of Easter*, the ambiguous image of Osiris-Christ is used to accent beliefs and practices in society that do not come with a true and deeply understood tradition. Such practices are deemed fraudulent and self-deceiving, representative of individuals and societies indulging in charades. The *Temple Caves* series seem to dwell deep in a human consciousness that grapples with the understanding and expression of spirituality. The acknowledgement of these inadequacies is in itself a discovery which is both painful and therapeutic. However, the apprehension and ambiguity over one's spirituality does not result in complete despair, but opens up little fractures of hope without which it would be impossible to carry on living.

Ideas reflecting social and ideological constraints erected by society are further extended in the series *From Chairil Anwar (1922–1949)*. They depict situations where the individual rebels against state and societal apparatus that curbs freedom of action and thought. The Indonesian poet's concern of dismantling romantic attachments to conservative attitudes seem to aptly suit the agenda of Wong's in this collection.

As with his earlier poems and collections, Wong's latest collection, *Against the Wilderness* attempts to capture the immigrant sensibility and minority consciousness. The opening sequence of twelve sonnets sounds the voices of Chinese immigrants to Malaysia. They chart immigrant consciousness from China, across the seas, to old Malacca, the jungles, the tin mines, through the fear for survival to the wilderness of modernised Malaysia. "Antecedent" describes the immigrants' "nightmarish" life in China, which reduced them to despair:

> When people turned from eating bark to sand, we waited
> For our dead to putrefy before we buried them.

>   (2000, p. 3)

The immigrants' desperate search for redemption was not for want but need, and so they left with only hope in heart. When all attempts of finding sanctuary at home fails, they board the junks and sail the high seas. *Bukit China (1)* describes this journey away from home as not simply a physical one. The persona says:

> I became a stranger beast . . . Chopper in hand,
> I worked through rib cage and skull, through
> settled, bleeding men
> As I would shake from me this pain, this
> abandonment by spirit.

(2000, p. 4)

The hope that sustains their journey acquires new vigour at the thought of finding a new home that promises security and comfort. *Bukit China (2)* reflects this immigrant dream:

> My flesh would find continuance in the moist salt wombs
> of native women and leave secreted into this hill
> a clutch of bones from which no transfigured life would
> hatch.

(2000, p. 5)

The *Arrival* to the new land is both shocking and welcoming. The intimacy between the "sun" and the "habour", the "alight wharves", the "oiled sea smells" and the "gibberish" language all serve to awaken the immigrant to a living world, so strange to their spirit. But even here a premonition of what is to be seems apparent:

> I saw that sailing in,
> Jungle pouring out of mountains into sea's mouth,
> holding the world's gloom, its inhospitable spirit.

(2000, p. 6)

This series of sonnets delve deep into the Chinese immigrant psyche bring to surface their problems, fear, anxiety and resistance they encounter in coming to terms with the new environment. They demonstrate the difficulty of the first generation's plight in searching for a sense of belonging. Yet the fear of not belonging and not being wanted remains strong. They cling to tradition and culture as warm coats that protect them against social and psychological fears.

China Bride depicts one such clinging, where the early Chinese settlers bring from the Chinese mainland women to be their brides. This may be seen as attempts to preserve and survive within a known and secure cultural garrison.

This painful journey of the immigrant is also charted to capture the consciousness of the generations after. Their destiny takes them from the coast through the jungles to the rivers to emerge in the cities. These sonnets do not present this journey as a pleasant one. If China had been desperate and devastating, then resettlement heart wrenching and painful. The pressures came from within and without. The final sonnet in this series, "A field not mine", depicts that the only way the immigrant can come to terms with his environment is through cultural references ingrained in him.

> Yet in darkness most profound
> Beneath the flooded field, not mine, the dragon stirs.
>
> (2000, p. 14)

The complex and contrasting conditions of wants and needs, belonging and not belonging, of identity and hybridity continues. Modernisation and material life has not eased the search for self. It has simply added more spikes and barbs to tread over, across a more globalised social and cultural minefield.

Wong's poems write a wasteland representing a troubled minority consciousness. The motifs of desperation and desolation are repeated time and again to emphasise destitution in the minority psyche in search of self, identity, sense of belonging and a place to belong. The views of Lloyd Fernando, another of Malaysia's eminent creative writers in English lend support to Wong's depictions:

> Every Malaysian of "immigrant" stock must go through an exhausting process of unlearning, besides undertaking to learn with his instincts the native culture and traditions of his new country. Only those who are aware of this dual process of unlearning and learning know the degree of spiritual labour they will have to embrace... It is as if every nerve and fibre must be undone and laid bare before being reassembled in an apter way.
>
> (1986, p. 45)

3.3 Conclusion

The two most remarkable features of Wong Phui Nam's poetry are the seriousness of attitude in the intent they display and the care with which they are crafted. For the most parts, the poetry manifests an admirable synthesis of diction, structure and imagery, a quality that allows interpretations within both literal and metaphorical dimensions. Wong Phui Nam's poems seem to be more than literary art. They appear as social and historical documents that capture the many emotions and experience of a nation in growth. They boldly embody the perceptions and perspectives a major voice of that nation, the voice of the minority-immigrant Chinese in Malaysia. His poems explore and question the issues of identity, hybridity, sense of belonging and national identity. They express a pain that comes with an unending search, inhibited by conditions, artificially imposed. In spite of their excellent craftsmanship, Wong poems cannot hide the sadness and gloom they epitomise. The poems seem to capture in their nakedness some of the bitter realities of life from which we attempt to hide. Wong's message seems to be that the truth however painful, has to be faced —understood and accepted, for only then can inroads be made towards creating a truly Malaysian people with a single and national identity.

The work of Wong Phui Nam both as a poet and critic have had significant impact on the Malaysian literary scene. His sharp yet insightful criticism of many local and foreign creative works have lead to fruitful and in-depth debates which have only served to enrich the Malaysian literary scenario. His poetry, which parodies, the self, and society is enriched by conventions seemingly of 19th century English fiction and the use of mimicry. He exemplifies a craft beyond the use of "native" form and colour, to that of native sensibilities and poetics. Wong Phui Nam is a poetic craftsman before a bearer of concerns and his concerns will be effective without the craft.

Bibliography

Chin, O. P. & Tan, P. (1995). *Enigma in exile*. Unpublished interview with Wong Phui Nam, School of Language Studies and Linguistics, Faculty of Social Sciences and Humanities, Universiti Kebangsaan Malaysia.

Subramaniam, G. (1995). *Desolate in exile: Reflections on the poetry of Wong Phui Nam*. Kuala Lumpur: Universiti Kebangsaan Malaysia.

Wong, P. N. (1957/58). Irrationality, Images, Afternoon, The Covenant and Sum in *30 Poems: University of Malaya poems 1957–1958*

———. (1958). Blood panned out in tissues of the brain, Moment, African Tulip, Pollens in the brain throw roots and burgeon, Amoeba, Nocturne, Ritual, Mimosa, Sentience is gestated and Hibiscus. In *Litmus one: Selected university verse, 1949–1957*. Singapore: Raffles Society, University of Malaya.

———. (1958). *Tocatta on ochre sheaves*. Singapore: Raffles Society, University of Malaya

———. (1964). Prospect of spring and Candles for a local Osiris in *Tumasek, 11*, (n.p.) (Republished in *Poet:Singapore and Malaysia Number 1*).

———. (1964). How the hills are distant, A version from T'ao Yuan Ming and Nocturne and Bagatelles(selections). In T. Wignesan (ed.), *Bunga emas: An anthology of contemporary Malaysian literature* (n.p.) London: Anthony Blond with Rayirath (Raybooks) Publications Malaysia.

———. (1966). Images and afternoon. In A. L. McLoed (ed.), *Malaysian literature in English*. Honolulu: University of Hawaii Press.

———. (1968). My uncle dying. *Tenggara, 2*(1), (n.p).

———. (1968). Remembering grandma. *Tenggara, 2*(1), (n.p).

———. (1968). How the hills are distant. *Tenggara* (Supplement). Department of English, Universiti Malaya.

————. (1970). African tulip, Poem for a birthday, Words for Easter, A death in ward 13 and Prospect in Spring. In E. Thumboo (ed.), *The Flowering Tree*. Singapore: Educational Publications Bureau, Ministry of Education Singapore.

————. (1971). For my old Amah. *Westerly, 3,*(n.p.) (Republished in *Remembering grandma and other rumours.*)

————. (1973). Prospect in spring, Candles for a Local Osiris, Poem for a birthday and Words for easter. In Edwin Thumboo (ed.), *Seven poets*. Singapore: Singapore University Press.

————. (1988). Poem for a birthday, A death in ward 13, Stepmother and Cousin. In K. S. Maniam and M.Shanmughalingham (eds.), *An anthology of Malaysian poetry*. Kuala Lumpur: Dewan Bahasa dan Pustaka.

————. (1989). *Remembering grandma and other rumours*. Kuala Lumpur: Department of English Language and Literature, National University of Singapore.

————. (1993). *Ways of exile*. London: Skoob Books Publishing Ltd.

————. (1993). Terminal Ward. In C. Y. Loh and I. K. Ong (eds.), *Southeast Asia writes back! Skoob Pacifica anthology No. 1* (pp. 175–178). London: Skoob Books Publishing Ltd.

————. (1993). Poems of Chairil Anwar. In C. Y. Loh and I. K. Ong (eds.), *Southeast Asia writes back! Skoob Pacifica anthology No. 1* (pp. 278–282). London: Skoob Books Publishing Ltd.

————. (1994). A God drowns. In C. Y. Loh and I. K. Ong (eds.), *The pen is mightier than the sword. Skoob Pacifica anthology No. 2* (pp. 115). London: Skoob Books Publishing Ltd.

————. (1994). A Fire Easter. In C. Y. Loh and I. K. Ong (eds.),*The pen is mightier than the sword. Skoob Pacifica anthology No. 2* (pp. 115–117). London: Skoob Books Publishing Ltd.

————. (2000). *Against the wilderness*. Kuala Lumpur: Blackwater Books.

Lee Kok Liang

4.0 Epigraph

Perhaps in these parts of the world we tend to treat art, culture, writing and other manifestations of human effort in the direction of creative activities a bit too seriously. There is certain earnestness about our behaviour—either we look at our writers, artists and composers, and other cultural bearers through the wrong end of the telescope or we tell them what they should or should not do. By we I imply the non-us that is the others of whom we form a part yet from whom we disassociate ourselves. We blame politicians, we ridicule beauracrats, we avoid the establishment. Partly it is because we feel that the politicians want us to write what they want us to. We feel also that the beauracrats can never understand us. We think of the establishment as being bourgeois, money-grabbers and unsympathetic. A conclave of writers meeting in Southeast Asia would understand the sentiments expressed above. And yet perhaps the fault lies in ourselves: we do not—what was it that Chekov wrote—"embrace politics in order to negate politics".

— Lee Kok Liang
(1991, p. 1)

4.1 Introduction

Lee Kok Liang was born in 1927 in Sungai Petani, Kedah. He was a fifth-generation Chinese who lived in Penang for most parts of his life. He was educated in both Chinese and English. His primary school days were spent in Sungai Petani, following which his family moved to Penang. Here he went to Penang Free School and later, in his own words "took a reverse direction and went to Chung Ling

High School". He pursued his higher education in Melbourne University and this was where he first began to write. The first of Lee Kok Liang's work was published in 1949 in the university magazine when he was twenty-two.

On his return to Malaysia as a qualified lawyer, he started a law practice in Penang and later ventured into politics for a short while. He won the Tanjung State Assembly seat on a Labour party ticket and served for one term as a state assemblyman. In spite of this, Lee Kok Liang's passion for writing never ceased. He managed to juggle a successful law career, marriage, and his passion for writing remarkably well.

Lee Kok Liang wrote in English and drew his subjects for most parts from the immigrant Chinese community. His works have been published in a London magazine, the Melbourne University magazine, in collections of Commonwealth short stories, and in other journals and anthologies in the United Kingdom, Australia, Malaysia and the United States of America. He has written two novels, *Flowers in the Sky* and a posthumously published work, *London Does Not Belong to Me*. His novelette, *The Mutes in the Sun* was published together with other short stories. Another collection of his short stories is called *Death is a Ceremony*.

Aside from his writings, Lee Kok Liang has played his part in the development of Malaysian literature in English. He was Editorial Consultant of *Tenggara* from 1967 to1 969. He was also one of the judges in the *New Straits Times* Short Story Competition from 1987 to 1992, which paved the way for the emergence of many talented short story writers in the country.

Lee Kok Liang's death on December 24, 1992, on the eve of Christmas was sudden and unexpected. At that time of his death, he was in process of completing a collection tentatively called *The Magical Moments of Mollika*, a third compilation of short stories, and a book of "Fairy Tales for God Daughters" entitled *Ah Tong and the Horseface Princess*. *The Magical Moments of Mollika* was later published posthumously.

4.2   Discussion of works

Lee Kok Liang, inspite of being the fifth-generation Chinese in Malaysia, focused much on his works on the immigrant Chinese community. In the early immigration period, the Chinese community was communal and had a tendency to cluster together in their respective clans. Each individual within the clan would be very dependent on other members. According to Lee Kok Liang, such a social environment makes one look closely at the others within the community. The early works of the writer portray exactly this kind of situations. Lee Kok Liang derived inspiration from the social and physical environment. He readily admitted that much of his writing is based on personal experiences derived from his childhood and everything that went on around him. He took note of things that attract his attention and immediately makes "one-liners". He pondered over them later when he was writing and at times, these "one-liners" became a short story or a novel.

In spite of stating that his legal career had no influence over the way he wrote, it is quite evident that his works often raise questions of fair play. *Mutes in the Sun, The Glittering Game* and even *Ibrahim Something* focus on the issues of justice and injustice. But the writer never made judgements on the characters. That is left to the reader.

Lee Kok Liang had a liking for the works of Anton Chekov. In the racks of his law office sat a large collection of Chekov's work. Lee Kok Liang said he liked to read Chekov as much as any other writer, though he held Chekov's philosophy of freedom of expression close at heart. That, he claimed was the extent of Chekov's influence on him.

In his own words, Lee Kok Liang said that the only influence on his works were his experiences and the things that happened around him. He wrote because he wanted to, and because he hoped to "kindle a glow" in the hearts of his readers.

Lee Kok Liang's novels portrayed scenes of ordinary or everyday life, based on his own experiences and what he saw around him. Kee Thuan Chye (1992) comments, "The world he (Lee Kok

Liang) evoked were primarily those he knew intimately, often revolving around the Penang Hokkien community of which his family has been a part of for at least four generations."

The stories depicted in his novels are "capsules of his vision of his people" and important incidences of "a lifestyle, society's value system, beliefs and practices that change with time". However, for Lee Kok Liang, "the fundamentals of human nature remain the same, irrespective of what period his stories were set in" (Kee, 1992).

The characters in Lee Kok Liang's novels are portrayed as sufferers who are helplessly caught in the whirl of life. The kind of novel that Lee Kok Liang wrote were more of novels of characters rather than incidents, as the greater weight of interest is on what the character's motives are for what he does and on how the character will turn out. Lee Kok Liang employed a kind of "experimental style" where he constantly provided differing perceptions the personality of his characters. Lee Kok Liang also revealed that he experimented with various kinds of characters in his stories, based on the people he met or read about and developed them into full-blown characters when he wrote.

A classic example of this is found in *Flowers in the Sky*, a novel that charts the paths of progress of the two main characters, Venerable Hung and Surgeon K—one in search of spiritual enrichment, the other of material wealth. *Flowers in the Sky* is a novel of formation where the subject is structured around the development of Venerable Hung's and Mr. K's minds and characters, as they pass from childhood through varied experiences told in flashbacks, through a spiritual crisis, into maturity and the recognition of identity and role in life. Some of the events in this novel like the finding of the statue of Ganesh are real events reported in local newspapers some years ago.

Lee Kok Liang's novel and novella can also be classified as truly Malaysian novels as there are elements of local colour in the setting, speech, social structure and customs of a particular locality, which is Malaysia in general and Penang in particular. The specific conditions of locale and heritage are shown to affect the temperament, ways of thinking, feeling and interaction of his immigrant characters (Kwan-Terry, 1984).

In his novel, *Flowers in the Sky* and novella *The Mutes in the Sun*, Lee Kok Liang's concerns led him to view man as "a creature oppressed by loneliness, unable to articulate his dispossession; overwhelmed by a sense of inadequacy and bewilderment as he confronts a new environment; and grappling with the problem of finding a new accommodation as those familiar to his life and his experience are corroded"(Kwan-Terry, 1984, p. 155). These motifs are presented with comic detachment, yet the optimistic outlook is not at the expense of the tragic undertones of the novel.

The novel, *Flowers in the Sky* has a very loose plot. The plot reveals the diversity of manifestations of the essential oneness of the human desires for love and fulfilment with which each man has to wrestle in the solitariness of his private being (Kwan-Terry, 1984). The nature of man's estate is performed through a series of overlapping antinomies, which either assume the form of paradoxes or are precariously reconciled through the element of chance. The characters live in the world that constantly invades their senses, but they only "see" and do not "feel".

The Mutes in the Sun and *Flowers in the Sky* display many of the naturalistic techniques, which include a precise use of regional or localized details and colour. They are written in a narrative method, which creates a sense of realism, in the portrayal of characters.

There are similarities in the narrative technique employed and in the titles between *Flowers in the Sky* and *The Mutes in the Sun*. However, one obvious difference is in the use of time. The time-shifts in *The Mutes in the Sun* are vaguely indicated, while the time frame in the *Flowers in the Sky* is very explicit and forms the basis for the sections, with thirteen divisions of varying lengths from "3.00 p.m. Wednesday" through to "10.00 a.m. Monday". This exhibits features of literary realism, which are visible in Lee Kok Liang's writings in which he uses narrative techniques that relate to theme, local colour and point of view.

Lee Kok Liang wrote his novels based on his psychic sensibilities and out of interest, but claimed not to have selected the topic, theme or plot deliberately. The first thing that Lee Kok Liang would do was to come up with "one-liners" when an idea struck him. Then, he would go through a "gestation period". This is when he would think and plan hi writing. He would also read about the topic, conduct research into the environment of the characters in order to provide sufficient dimension or depth to his characters. He ascribed this to be the reason for taking a long time to write *Flowers in the Sky*.

Based on the number of short stories he had written, it may be claimed this literary genre is his preferred medium of literary expression. His first collection of short stories is entitled *The Mutes in the Sun and Other Stories*, and his second collection is *Death is a Ceremony*. A collection of his short stories was also published in Lloyd Fernando's *Twenty-two Malaysian Stories*.

Most of Lee Kok Liang's works may be considered anecdotal as the short stories are often simple and unelaborated narrations of a single incident. His stories organise the action, thought and interaction of the characters into the pattern of a plot. The plot the story has a beginning and develops through a middle to some sort of denouement at the end. The plot includes the elements of comedy, tragedy, romance and even satire.

Lee Kok Liang's works are examples of realism and naturalism. The narrative elements in his stories make them vivid and realistic. One element of narration found in many of his short stories is the use of dialogue. The delightful use of local dialect, as in *Return to Malaya*, is another of technique of realism. Apart from these, *Five Fingers* is full of details of the Chinese-Malaysian life, as are *The Pei-Pa*, *Ami To Fu* and *The Glittering Game*. The details are also drawn from the visible world of British Malaya, or more accurately Penang under British rule where Lee Kok Liang spent most of his life.

Lee Kok Liang's short stories dwell on the minds of his characters. *Five Fingers*, *The Pei-Pa*, *Birthday* and *Ami To Fu* are stories, which depict a world that is self-enclosed, like a community under siege, fighting for survival and to keep its character intact (Kwan-Terry, 1984).

His short stories can be read at one sitting and is limited to "a certain unique or single effect" to which every detail is subordinate. This is what Edgar Allan Poe defined as "the prose talk". Lee also introduces a very few characters in a story as his stories afford little space for leisurely analysis or to develop the story in detail as a novelist would have been able to. He often begins a story close to, or even on the verge of the climax. This makes his short stories exciting to read.

Lee Kok Liang cleverly combines effective writing techniques and appropriate language use in order to convey the ideas and messages in the stories. Although his stories revolve around the people and places most familiar to him, such as the immigrants Chinese in Penang, he managed to represent the life of Malaysian people in general as well as portray the universal truth of the human race.

Basically, Lee Kok Liang's stories are derived from his keen and careful observation of the people and situation around him. His favourite subjects and characters are people from the lower strata of society: the poor and the physically handicapped such as the mutes in *The Mutes in the Sun* and *Flowers in the Sky*. In his attempt to highlight the predicament of such people against the harshness of the real world, Lee Kok Liang presents his characters ironically. For instance, the mute girl, Ah Lan in *Flowers in the Sky* actually evokes the monk's sexual awareness, which he tries very hard to deny. However, Lee Kok Liang is compassionate and highly sensitive in describing his characters. One critic, Syd Harrex (1982) identifies Lee Kok Liang's writing style as a "creative blend of irony and compassion; providing a dual focus, conducive to objectivity" (p. 2) and very appropriate to the Malaysian context.

The essence of Lee Kok Liang's narratives is his ability to provide a vivid description of characters and events. His powerful and creative imagination on subjects familiar to him allows realistic presentations of the characters and events. In *Return to Malaya*, Lee Kok Liang painted a vivid scene of the country with its exotic local images. Kwan-Terry (1984) acknowledges Lee Kok Liang's ability to provide "a visual intensity in explicating emotion in concrete image" such as through "localised landscape which has public significance". Another critic, Wood (1988) refers to Lee Kok Liang's writing style as a realistic representation of life and naturalistic portrayal of character. She further comments on the "abundance of descriptive details" such as the characters clad in sarong and singlet indicative of the Malaysian culture and environment. Harrex (1982) also observes that Lee Kok Liang's narratives preserve the Malaysian "flavours, tones and textures" to create a "sense of contemporary" to represent that "Malaysian time, place and character".

Lee Kok Liang's presentation of character is, to a certain extent, controlled by the themes of the story. Dumb, Dumb in *Dumb, Dumb by a Bee Stung* signifies the alienation of the handicapped person. However, Lee Kok Liang did not provide any explanation as to the cause of the character's muteness nor conclusions to his predicament. In fact, many of the stories often end without a conclusion. Harrex (1982) calls this technique of withdrawing unstated or instated facts as "restricted focus or incomplete vision" (p. 2). It is appropriately used to represent the inconclusive nature of life. Furthermore, it allows creative and critical interpretations on the readers' part. Abdul Majid Nabi Baksh (1984) proposes that Lee Kok Liang uses this technique to captivate and sustain the readers' attention with the promise of "revelation in the near future". However, it must be noted that Lee Kok Liang's writing is spontaneous rather than didactic. This is essentially because his stories are meant only to create a kind of realisation.

Another prominent technique employed by the writer is the interior monologue, in which he operates from the minds of his characters. In his novel, *Flowers in the Sky*, the internal conflicts of Venerable Hung and Mr. K are displayed through their distinct thoughts in the forms of flashbacks and interior monologue. In this respect, the writer is almost omniscient in that he has the liberty to exploit the minds of his characters. According to Abdul Majid (1984), Lee Kok Liang's narratives are categorised into two main frames: "the objective or external world and the internal frame which includes interior monologue" (p. 11). The double frame is inter-changeable and is affected by the ideas intended. Through the interior monologue, the characters actually reveal the impact, which the objective world and that of the associated events have on them.

Elements of digression in the interior monologue also contribute to the dreamlike effect of the story. The events are presented not in chronological order yet quiet effectively, as it gives the characters a humanistic nature. Mr. K's (*Flowers in the Sky*) flashbacks of his past such as of his childhood and of his insecurities help to make him seem more human, thus deserving the readers' sympathy. Lee Kok Liang's clever manipulation of the flashback technique allows the smooth transition from the present to the past.

Harrex (1982) highlights that the sub-plots, which seem to lack coherence against the larger narrative actually serve to emphasise the main idea of the story. Interestingly, Lee Kok Liang seems to have very little concern for names of his characters and places. For example, the surgeon in *Flowers in the Sky* is only known as "Mr. K". Wood (1988) suggests that Lee Kok Liang deliberately uses this technique in order to associate whatever emotions and behaviours depicted, with all humankind and therefore making the philosophies explored, universal.

In spite of dealing with complex human concerns in his works, the language used by the writer is simple and straightforward. He gave a direct and vivid account of events and characters. Abdul Majid (1984) views Lee Kok Liang's language as "delicate, ethereal and almost ephemeral" as it gives a sense of realism to the description. The words are carefully and appropriately selected to signify the central theme of the story. The titles, *The Mutes in the Sun* correlates with the stories about the mutes and their predicaments, whereas *Flowers in the Sky* indicates the trance-like quality of the unfulfilled life of the monk as well as the surgeon. Similarly, Lee Kok Liang seems to prefer words that refer to nature or the cosmic such as "flowers", "sky", and "sun" pertinent to the serious and universal interest of the stories. His narratives often lack dialogues, which further emphasises the silent world of the mutes. Abdul Majid (1984) also points out that the language Lee Kok Liang used in his narratives is generally "evocative and dreamlike" yet not totally isolated from reality. Kee Thuan Chye (1992, p. 33) notes the writer's strength is in "his ability to powerfully suggest with an economy of expression". He views Lee Kok Liang's writing as "invariably vivid without being overly descriptive, Spartan yet succulent". Hence, Lee Kok Liang's writing style may be described as mature, bold and confident.

Lee Kok Liang's works are caricatures of social awareness in a multiracial nation. Many of his stories reflect the realisation of personal incompleteness. This theme is explored more subtly with keener psychological depth and greater dramatic effect. *Its All in Dream, Ibrahim Something, When the Saints Go Marching* and *Not So Long Ago But Still Around* all reflect this common theme. Here the characters' inner conflicts colours their moral perceptions to changed realities. His writings view man from various aspects:

> . . . a creature oppressed by loneliness, unable to articulate
> his dispossession, as someone overwhelmed by a sense
> of inadequacy and bewilderment as he confronts a new

environment and as someone grappling with the problem of finding a new accommodation as the familiar structures of his life and experience are corded . . .

(Kwan–Terrry, 1984, p. 154)

Harrex (1982) subsumes all these themes into a central and ubiquitous one: the enigma of identity. His concern with characters in his novels and short stories develop more personal and individualised themes. In *Flowers in the Sky,* themes of the vulnerability of the flesh, unfulfilment, and materialism as opposed to spiritualism permeate the story. Man's inability to cope with life is reflected by both physical and emotional muteness. It depicts the stifling of emotions and senses as seen in *Five Fingers, The Glittering Game, Just a Girl* and *Renggeng-Ronggeng*. The characters seem helpless against greed, exploitation, oppression, sexual repression, and societal norms.

Return to Malaya, reflects an identity crisis one which Lee Kok Liang himself admits to have faced as a young man returning home after reading law. It is a theme representative of the new generation of educated youth caught in an internal dilemma between new knowledge and a "stagnant" way of life. The inability to communicate again reflects muteness and the "loss of the bicycle" may depict the lost link with traditional values. In fact, this inability to cope with change is also present in *Death is a Ceremony* and *Dumb, Dumb by a Bee Stung.*

In general, the major themes portrayed in Lee Kok Liang's works reflect the conflicts that an individual faces as a result of both internal and external change, the struggle to cope with unfulfilled desires and the search for them. His works are important document of lifestyle, systems of values beliefs and practices that are changing with time" (Kee Tuan Chye, 1992, p. 33).

On December 1992, Kee Tuan Chye wrote, "Lee Kok Liang was in the forefront of his first generation of Malaysian creative writers in English" (p. 33). Both T. S. Wignesan and Lloyd Fernando (1968) considered him one of the foremost writers of English fiction in Malaysia. To many he was an excellent storyteller and a stylist. This acclaimed position was awarded to him because of his contribution to Malaysian literature in English from the 1960s to the early 1990s.

Lee Kok Liang was not tutored as a writer. Writing was his passion, which he pursued from his early university days in Melbourne, Australia. The publishing of his articles and stories in the university magazine motivated him to continue writing. In spite of being educated abroad, his heart and soul is very much Malaysian. Though most of his early works were primarily those he knew intimately, usually evolving around the immigrant Chinese community, his ideas and themes reflected a truly Malaysian worldview. In this sense, he was original. In spite of this, Kwan-Terry (1984, p. 161) says, "the question of significance of Lee Kok Liang's fiction, resting as it does on its representations of Malaysian time, place and characters, is complicated by the fact that Lee Kok Liang wrote in a country which has acknowledged national literature in Malay and several sectarian literatures written in Tamil, Chinese and English". Even so, Lee Kok Liang's fiction shares with mainstream Malay literature a common vision of the human predicament in a changing world depicting the changes faced by the immigrant communities or the nation as a whole after Independence.

He successfully evokes not only the texture and feel of Malaysian life but also a broad and integrated picture of multiracial Malaysia as a whole. Furthermore, it is significant that his works achieve an exactness of a localised landscape. Lee Kok Liang also dwelled in the political reality in some of his short stories, subtly providing a vision of the delicate political environment in the country. His works covered all aspects of Malaysian life; social cultural, political, economic, public, private, emotional and psychological all of which go towards understanding "the balance between the demands of idealism and the limitations of present day life" and "harmonising ourselves with a nation and its history, making ourselves more authentic than synthetic" (Kwan-Terry, 1984). On the whole, Lee Kok Liang's fiction presents a collage of life, culture, psychology and values of contemporary Malaysian society.

Lee Kok Liang led the way and set an example through his artistic accomplishments. Wood (1988) includes in this style "a precise use of regional details, local colour, a narrative method which created an exacting sense of realism and a deterministic portrayal of character usually described as naturalism". He introduced interior monologue in his works, and this was later refined by future generation of writes such as K.S. Maniam.

Ee Tiang Hong once said, "Among the few who attempted with any success to portray the linguistic and culture diversity of Malaysian, who have something to say about the human condition, and who say it with more then a passing interest, indeed, his interest was truly Malaysia," and his passing is a great loss to literature in Malaysia.

The significance of Lee Kok Liang's contributions is aptly highlighted with the posthumous publication of his first novel (2003), a novel Lee himself did not try to get published in his lifetime. The novel *London Does Not Belong to Me* was written when Lee Kok Liang was still a student in Britain. Edited by Syd Harrex and Bernard Wilson, the novel deals with the life of a Malaysian protagonist in a western setting. The significance of this novel, and Lee Kok Liang's works in general, are accurately expressed by another celebrated Malaysian writer, K.S. Maniam:

> Lee Kok Liang has always been for the leading literary figure, writing in English, in Malaysia. When writers taking up the craft in the language looked for guidance and inspiration, they invariably came to his writing. I was no exception... Writers in English, in Malaysia, have gone through painful experiences, publicly visible, to dissociate themselves from the influences of traditional British literature has had on them. They have had to go through

literary struggles, fairly consciously, and against an inherited sense of canonical values—education during the British times making them easy victims—to find their own voices. Lee seems to have done the reverse: he has attempted to enter a Eurocentric consciousness (in *London Does Not Belong to Me*) in order to find himself as a writer.

(2003, n.p)

4.3 Conclusion

The true reflections of Lee Kok Liang's works and life are echoed in the beliefs he expressed at a writers' conference in Singapore (see epigraph). In places and countries where creative writing and politics are intricately and inevitably tangled by institutional and constitutional designs, it is necessary for the creative writer not to simply question politics but to engage it manifestations into dialogue. Lee Kok Liang has done this in ways that are unique to him. He was among the group of pioneer Malaysian writers to write in English, who not only engaged in writing creatively in a language not his own, but moulded the language to embody the culture and sensibilities of the local landscape. He challenged the conventional tendencies to write and operate within the politically acceptable notions racial, cultural, and religious polarisation and isolation by writing about the multicultural and multiracial Malaysia engaging in everyday activities. His works expressed and drew awareness to the fears, anxieties and challenges faced by common people. Hence, Lee Kok Liang cannot be defined as a political writer in the conventional sense—one who either supports or challenges the establishment. His own personal involvement in politics had more than educated him in the deficiencies and inadequacies of politics. Therefore, Lee Kok Liang worked on with politics by engaging and expressing national consciousness of the common people.

Bibliography

Abdul Majid bin Nabi Baksh. (1984). Theme and technique in Lee Kok Liang's Flower in the sky. *Southeast Asian Review of English, 9*, (pp.16.)

Abrahms, M. H. (1981). *A glossary of literary terms* (4th ed.). New York: Holt, Reinhart and Winston.

Fernando, L. (ed.). (1968). *Twenty-two Malaysian stories: An anthology of writing in English.* Singapore: Heinemann Asia.

Harrex, S. C. (1982). Scalpel, scar, icon: Lee Kok Liang's "Flower in the sky". In B. Bennett *et. al* (eds.), *The writer's sense of the contemporary: Papers in Southeast Asian and Australian literature* (n.p). Nedlands: University of Western Australia.

Kee, T. C. (1992, December). (Lifestyle/Literary section). *The New Starits Times,* (p. 33).

Kwan-Terry, J. (1984). Narration and the structure of experience: The fiction of Lee Kok Liang. In C. E. Nicholson & R. Chatterjee (eds.), *Tropic crucible: Self and* theory in language and literature (pp. 143–162). Singapore: National University Press.

Lee, K. L. (1981). *Flowers in the sky.* Kuala Lumpur: Heinemann Educational Books (Asia) Ltd.

————. (1991). *The mutes in the sun and other stories.* Singapore:Federal Publications (S) Pte. Ltd. (First published in 1964)

————. (1992). *Death is a ceremony and other short stories.* Singapore: Federal Publications (S) Pte. Ltd.

Subramaniam, G. *et al.* (1992). Unpublished interview with Lee Kok Liang. Faculty of Education, Universiti Putra Malaysia.

Wood, S. (1988). Silence, communication and cultural conflict in Lee Kok Liang's The mutes in the sun and Flowers in the sky. *Tenggara,* (pp. 88–103.)

Cecil Rajendra

5.0 Epigraph

The sad thing about the world today is that in spite of our tremendous resources, incredible technology, the ending of cold wars etc... life for the majority of people on this planet remains abysmal. Millions go hungry every night, are homeless, victims of innumerable wars, famine and diseases, both old and new such as Ebola and AIDS. When I see or hear of these injustices in a world of plenty when such things can be cured, circumvented or avoided I get hopping mad, especially when the victims are innocent children.

And I am forced to bare my teeth not only as a therapeutic exercise to keep my rancour in check but hopefully also stir someone out there to get equally angry and do something about our miserable situation. I am a great believer in what Seamus Heaney calls the redress of poetry and am firmly convinced that poetry has a role to play in redressing the imbalances of the world.

— Cecil Rajendra
(1996, p. 31)

5.1 Introduction

Like many other creative writers in Malaysia, Cecil Rajendra is not a full-time poet. Although he has about thirteen volumes of poetry published, he is a lawyer by profession. He practises in Penang, where he actively handles free legal aid to serve needy people who normally have no access to legal representation. Naturally, this altruistic characteristic is carried through in his poetry. Describing himself as a "radical humanis", Rajendra's poetry is mostly concerned with issues such as war, poverty, social injustice and environmental devastation. Although he also writes love poetry as exemplified in *Eros and Ashes*, Rajendra is primarily known for his passion for championing social ills.

Rajendra was born in Penang and spent the best part of his childhood in the fishing village of Tanjong Tokong, which has now been dismantled in the name of progress and development. He received his formal education in St. Xavier's Institution, Penang, the University of Singapore and Lincoln's Inn, London where he qualified as a Barrister-at-Law in 1968. During his thirteen-year stay in London, Rajendra worked in a variety of jobs including as a cook, postal worker, messenger, labourer, a wine cellar porter, youth officer, scriptwriter, market researcher and legal advisor. Being acquainted with jobs at first menial and later on, professional, contributed to making Rajendra a multifaceted man who is knowledgeable of people at the periphery as well as at the centre of society.

In the early 1970s, he initiated a highly successful Third World Cultural Forum called "Black Voices" in the basement of the Troubadour Coffee House, in old Brampton Road, London. During its run the forum played host to a galaxy of budding and major Third World writers and poets including Walter Rodney, Edward Kamau Braithwaite, Dennis Brutus, Mahmood Jamal, Andrew Salkey, James Berry and Linton Kwesi Johnson.

At this time too Rajendra teamed up with Cecil Roberts (Sierra Leone) and Hello Diaz Pinto (Brazil) to form the unique and groundbreaking Troubadours—a travelling group of players who used the medium of poetry and music to bear dynamic witness to the situation in developing countries. While residing in London, Rajendra was the first Malaysian poet to be listed by the National Poetry Secretariat of Great Britain and Northern Ireland as well as the London Poetry Secretariat.

5.2   Discussion of works

His collection of works surpasses thirteen volumes, a corpus larger than any other Malaysian poets' works in English. His publications include *Embryo* (1965), *Eros & Ashes* (1975), *Bones & Feathers* (1978), *Refugees & Other Despairs* (1980), *Hour of Assassins* (1983), *Songs for the Unsung* (1983), *Postscripts* (1984), *Child of the Sun* (1986), *Dove on Fire* (1987), *Lovers Lunatics & Lallang* (1989), *Papa Moose's Nursery Rhymes for Our Times* (1991), *Zerbrochene Traume* (1992) and *Broken Buds* (1994). His poems have been published and broadcast in many countries and translated into several languages including Japanese, Chinese, Tamil, Urdu, Bengali, German, Malay, Tagalog, Danish, Dutch and Spanish. Because of the nature of Rajendra's poetry, which touches on many sensitive issues, and the speed in which his works get published, Rajendra's career as a poet is hardly acknowledged in Malaysia. Rajendra himself says that his "poems tend to be more a part of Third World studies than literature studies" (Addison, 1982, n.p). This book acknowledges Rajendra as a major creative figure. No local publisher or distributor will handle his books and local literary circles avoid him. Local critics are especially harsh:

> The next time you step into a shoe shop and find the salesman earnestly practising his rhetoric on you on the excellence of his wares, you will be safe in concluding that Rajendra is doing more or less the same thing in his poems. The difference between the two, if you choose to see the difference, is the difference between the one trying to sell shoes as a legitimate ambition and the other deceiving himself into thinking that he is spouting poetry to save the world when he is really making a desperate plea for approbation. Most people will enjoy a little attention but who would care to go to such laughable extremes to get it.
>
> (Wong Phui Nam, 1992, n.p)

Wong Phui Nam touches on the seeming insincerity of Rajendra's poems, because Rajendra seems bent on bringing repeatedly to the fore issues which may appear to be the same. While Rajendra may touch on many issues ranging from free speech to environment, his personas' tone do not change. All of them are straight-forward—one need not read in between the lines to understand the persona's stance towards an issue. Rajendra probably does not believe in art for art's sake because he judges his work strictly in terms of its effectiveness in awakening people to the burning social issues that afflict Malaysia and the Third World generally—oppression, injustice and exploitation, corruption and greed, want, hunger and poverty, ecological ruin" (Addison, 1982, n.p).

Contrary to the belief of many, Rajendra's concern is prevalent in the writings of Malaysian writers. The issue on pollution, for example, is tackled by A. Samad Said in his poem *The Dead Crow*, which has been included as a part of the national syllabus. In the poem, the persona condemns the politicians for their lack of concern over the matter, very similar to Rajendra's own stand on environmental issues. Thus, it would be wrong to argue that Rajendra's unceasing passion for high moral ground is not genuine. It would be our cultural loss to deny Rajendra his place in Malaysian literature in English. His honest, perhaps brutal way of confronting many social ills may cause discomfort; his simple, no-frills language may not seem poetic, and the speed in which his volumes of poetry appear on the market is astounding but Rajendra's mission as a poet in charting imperfections in his homeland and elsewhere should be considered in a good light. He does not put poetry on a pedestal; by being non-elitist, Rajendra's poems have the capacity to touch people from all walks of life.

His style is very much influenced by the American modernist poet, T.S. Eliot and Japanese haiku poetry, characterised by concise and concentrated imagery; his thinking is influenced by Amilcar Cabral, Pablo Neruda, Franz Fanon, Walter Rodney, Martin Luther King, Malcolm X, Wilfred Owen and Dennis Brutus. As Conrad Taylor states, Rajendra is not the typical Malaysian poet:

> His poems, often angry and impassioned, reflect a
> burning concern about social injustice. Generally

partisan and political, they run counter to mainstream Malaysian verse which, according to the poet, tends to be more preoccupied with form than relevance and is predicated on an ideal of poet as sympathetic but distant observer of human suffering and ecstasy—a combination of Taoist sage and English country squire.

(1979, p. 62)

By attacking Malaysian writers for this lethargy in making visible social ills, the Malaysian literary scene does not look upon Rajendra's works kindly. As Taylor has maintained, what Rajendra believes in is age-old bickering between two kinds of art—art-for-art's sake and art being polemical and pedagogical.

His first collection of poems, entitled *Embryo* (1965) was indeed very embryonic in nature. After getting bad reviews, Rajendra did not publish anything until 1972 when he edited a volume of black poetry titled *Other Voices, Other Places*. The same year, he organised Black Voices Forum in an old coffee house-cum-folk club (The Troubadour) on London's Brompton Road to facilitate exchanges among Africans, Asian and Latin American poets, musicians and activists. Out of the forum sprang the Third World Troubadours, a group that delivered poetry to "the people"; Rajendra recited poems (mostly his own), accompanied by guitar or piano and drums. The group made extensive and successful tours, reaching beyond the black community to British and North American universities with its message of protest at injustice around the world.

Rajendra blossomed with public exposure and the feedback gained through direct encounters with a live audience. His verse developed strong informal rhythms and vivid imagery. His lines built up tension, like oratory, sometimes coming to powerful climactic conclusions and sometimes veering off into the outrageous. Much of Rajendra's poetry from this period was created for aural consumption and to read those poems in silence is sometimes akin to reading a musical score; in both cases, much power and beauty is lost.

In an interview, Rajendra argues that poets are supposed to be sensitive. He takes it further—by penning sensitive issues afflicting the Third World. The fact that publishers overseas readily publish his works has caused some consternation among local writers, much of this connected with the view that the problems of the Third World are sources of exotica for Western consumption. But based on Rajendra's journey as poet, his passion for writing on Third World issues are not about orientalising his nation but a desire to raise his readers' conscience about balancing material development and spiritual contentment.

Ecological ruin is an issue close to Rajendra's heart. Ecological ruin covers many aspects — indiscriminate land clearing, emission of hazardous gases and land reclamation. In *Child of the Sun and other Poems*, poems such as *Ecological Suicide* and *A Prescription for Development*, Rajendra's personas are alarmed at the level of destruction wrought on his mother earth. *Ecological Suicide* describes environmental problems: choked and polluted river, and haze, which drive people away from their habitat. Pollution, the persona says, is brought about by the inhabitants themselves, "we are the authors of our death / our own nemesis" (*Child of the Sun*, p. 6). In his eleventh book, *Papa Moose's Nursery Rhymes for Our Times*, he derived the inspiration to compose it from his daughter. It is a revised version of traditional Mother Goose nursery rhymes that cover a wide spectrum of contemporary issues such as ecological ruin, corruption, justice and human rights. Many of the poems in this anthology may seem simple but the messages embedded in them are serious and worthy of attention. Rajendra transforms children's rhymes into poems about the environment. Rajendra's transformation can be described as re-visionary, a writing strategy popularised Adrienne Rich (1980). In re-visioning, a writer takes texts of the past and transforms them in the light of the present. Although Rich's purpose has a feminist impulse, her strategy has been adopted by other writers. By re-visioning, a writer jolts new perspectives using familiar texts and thus offers new alternatives to his/her readers.

Environmental issues are one of Rajendra's favourite concerns. One of the prominent points in environmental issues is forest preservation, which is not a utopian dream if there is a concerted effort and deep-rooted awareness in humankind to safeguard nature. Indiscriminate clearing of trees and hilltops has become more prevalent these days without considering the pernicious effects. This idea is perspicuously conveyed in *All the Trees Are Falling Down*, drawn from the rhyme *London Bridge Is Falling Down*.

A selection from *Papa Moose's Nursery Rhymes* was first previewed in *Environmental Directions*, the Los Angeles-based award-winning series, which was aired in over 25 million homes in four countries. Some of the rhymes were also presented by the author and Rama May at an international workshop, Workshop on Consumer Health, Drug Information and Education organised by the international Organisation of Consumers Unions. This shows that Rajendra's poems have wide international appeal because of the issues embedded in them. One such poem is entitled *Acid Rain, Acid Rain*:

> Acid rain,
> Acid rain,
> Go away!
> Don't come back
> On another day
> Or there'll never be
> Any children left to play.

(1991, n.p)

Taken from the children's rhyme *Rain, Rain, Go Away*, Rajendra gives his revision a new twist by reminding readers of not just any ordinary rain, but acid rain. He cautions against acid rain, caused by chemicals released in the air because of hazardous emission from vehicles, factories and other industrial units. These dangerous substances, when released irresponsibly into the air, will cause many problems to our society. Increased cases of asthma and cancer are some of the fatalities wrought by acid rain. His simple, catchy rhythmic pattern of repetition of acid rain and rhyming pattern of aabcbdb strikes a chord in the reader that acid rain will eventually kill all children on this earth. There will be no more happy chatter of "rain, rain, go away" when acid rain becomes a permanent phenomenon on earth.

Another poem concerning the fatal AIDS goes like this:

> Georgie, HIV-posi
> Was condom-shy
>> He kissed the girls
>> And made them die
>
> So when you boys
> Go out to play
>> Do not forget
>> It's AIDS doomsday

(1991, n.p)

This poem, re-visioned from *Georgie Porgie, Pudding and Pie* takes us to another aspect of modernity—liberal sex and its consequences. As Asians, we do not speak openly of indiscriminate sexual intercourse and its price on children, thinking that these things will sort themselves out when the children are older. But AIDS, a disease brought about by promiscuity and drug abuse, is a scourge, which must be hindered. Rajendra's poem is a fun and less sensitve way of reminding young readers of AIDS and what can be done to minimise contacting AIDS. In a jesting voice, Rajendra cautions his audience that sexual contact is not just for pleasure; it can bring about a lifetime of pain as well.

In *Peter, Wife-beater*, Rajendra describes a case of wife-battering, a more common phenomenon in Malaysia:

Peter, Peter, the wife-beater
Was served with a Court Order
From the Women's Crisis Centre
To keep well away from her.

He disobeyed that as well
And now sits in a prison cell!

(1991)

Wife beating is a domestic problem, which many women hide from public knowledge. An Asian society like ours adheres to the "save face" policy where airing dirty laundry in public amounts to violating the family honour. In order to keep family honour intact, many cases of wife battering and incest are family secrets. Rajendra's poems provide avenues for women to report cases of wife abuse, by going to court and keeping a distance from violent husbands. His law background is obvious here; his advice to women is that the law is here to protect them from further humiliation and danger.

Rajendra's poem called *Sa-Saddam and Bo-Bushie* raises another pertinent aspect of modernity—nuclear war. The poem goes like this:

Sa-Saddam and Bo-Bushie
Wanted to do battle
For Saddam, said Bushie
Has taken his oil barrel.
Into the fray came the UNO
With some sort of a resolution
That gave both our heroes the go—
Ahead for Global Devastation!

(1991, n.p)

In this poem, Rajendra was referring to the 1990 Bush-Saddam war as a result of Iraq's invasion of Kuwait. In 2002, another Gulf War erupted, led by US forces in coalition with Britain and Spain. The excuse was that Saddam had apparently amassed enough weapons of mass destruction. The United States shows its imperialistic head and bullies its way into invading Iraq without the sanction of the United Nations (UN). Rajendra highlights the destruction, which the war causes on the global scale. The number of lives lost in the first war—wives losing husbands, children losing parents and vice versa. The poet pokes fun at the UN for abandoning its principle of keeping peace among nations, and sneers at so-called Saddam and Bush for their short-term gain of popularity. While the heroes enjoy protection, the smaller beings are at the mercy of cannons and bombs. Rajendra's poem thus reminds us of the untold trauma on families and children which we do not get in the metanarrative of war.

Rajendra has been accused of being melodramatic on social issues. But judging from the sentiments poured out over the war on Iraq by the coalition forces, Rajendra's voice is not exaggerated. In an address at the opening session of the 13th Summit Meeting of the Non-Aligned Movement, the Prime Minister, Dato' Dr. Seri Mahathir Mohamad, made this remark:

The world now lives in fear. We are afraid of everything. We are afraid of flying, afraid of certain countries; afraid of bearded Asian men, afraid of shoes airline passengers wear; of letters and parcels, of white powder.

(*NST*, February 25, 2003, p. 10)

The sarcasm behind the repartee is close to Rajendra's attitude towards many things. His hatred for war is obvious in many poems, particularly *Twilight* (from *Broken Buds*):

The children
Haunt me most
At twilight

Twilight
Now turned to
Blood seeping

Through
Bandages of cloud
    Wrapped tight
Round
    The earth's brow
      As another

Wounded day
    Dies away
      Into the night

(1994, p. 31)

In another poem called *Radiation & the Rubaiyat*, Rajendra once again reminds his readers of the destruction caused by war:

And yes, i am too
Tired of protest.
O to be done
With this madness
And like Khayyam
Take to the wilderness
With a loaf of bread
A flask of wine
A book of verse
And a wild wild lass . . .

But now beneath
That nuclear
Bough, Omar
There's no paradise
The bread crumbles
To radioactive pieces
The wine is toxic
The maiden
  Leukemic

A skeleton
Screaming, not singing
In a wilderness
    Of ash.

(1994, n.p)

Certainly some of Rajendra's poems defy mainstream politics, attributed to his passion for pricking his society's social conscience. He feels for the alienated fisherman who has lost his source of livelihood because of encroachment of modernisation—the new highway, another seaside hotel. The image he paints of this man in *Fisherman's Tale*, from *Hour of Assassins* is sad:

Stealthily, at night
He descends to savour
The memories, to gaze
Across the now barren
Sea and to cast his hook and line of tears.

(1983, p. 46)

Love Poems

While poems that highlight social ills are dominant in Rajendra's writing, he also writes love poems. These writings, however, are of limited edition of only 500 copies.

Eros and Ashes describes a cycle of love poems written from the beginning to the end of a love affair. In 1982, the Kuala Lumpur Chamber Music Players under the segment *Season of Passion* featured this poem in their performance titled *Apollo God of Music & Poetry*. It is fitting that Rajendra's poetry can be accompanied by music because his use of rhythm highlights the fact that his poems are meant to be heard.

Eros & Ashes talks about love shared between a man and a woman. As childhood sweethearts, the two lovers are forced to go separate ways. But they meet again and renew their love affair albeit furtively. Doubts and regret haunt the relationship and once again they break up. The speaker however yearns and pines for his lover.

The title of this poem, *Eros & Ashes* is significant. Eros is the God of love in Greek Mythology representing passion. Ashes, on the other hand, is associated with the end of one's life. We see the contradiction between life and death as the speaker goes through life, love, hope, and eventually the burning out of the love of his life.

Two other collections of his love poems commemorate his love for his wife, Rebecca. Here we see another side of Rajendra, tender and warm, an antithesis to the often angry tone prevalent in his poems in his demands for social justice and political transparency. The poem (untitled) below illustrates this gentle persona:

> No filigree of words
> Can pin
> Your little presences
> Coiled
> In the interstices
> Of my bone . . .
>
> Spiralling out
> To press
> Against my brain
> In your absence

(1991, n.p)

The recurring sibilance found in "words", "interstices", "spiralling", "press" and "absence" convey gentle murmurings of love. His devotion is intoxicating—felt within his bones and savoured in his senses. The adulation may seem uncharacteristic of the angry personas of which with we often equate Rajendra.

5.3   Conclusion

Rajendra's works have sojourned far beyond the shores of Malaysia, and found a place in a wide variety of media forums; from anthologies to newspapers, journals, magazines, cassettes, records, posters, cantatas, radio and television programmes, an even the

UNESCO forum. They even incorporated his works in the school syllabus overseas. He remains Malaysia's most published poet. Being a man with a passion for truth, Rajendra sees his role as a poet to reaffirm and restate age-old obligations; the duty to speak up on behalf of those unable to do so. Until politicians carry out their responsibilities with a sense of purpose, until the hungry child is fed, until the battered woman gets help, until the environment is thriving, until social diseases no longer hog the headlines, Rajendra will continue to write his poetry.

Bibliography

Primary Texts

Rajendra, C. (1965). *Embryo*. UK: Regency Express.

———. (1975). *Eros & Ashes*. UK: Prakriti Press.

———. (1978). *Bones & feathers*. Place: Heinemann Educational Books (Asia) Ltd.

———. (1980). *Refugees & other despairs*. Singapore: Choice Books.

———. (1983). *Hour of assassins*. UK: Bogle L'Ouverture Publications.

———. (1983). *Songs for the unsung*. Geneva: WCC Publications.

———. (1984). *Postscripts*. Malaysia: Prai.

———. (1986). *Child of the sun*. UK: Bogle L'Ouverture Publications.

———. (1987). *Dove on Fire*. Geneva: WCC Publications.

———. (1989). *Lovers lunatics & lallang*. UK: BLP Publications.

———. (1989). *Bibliography and selected profiles, reviews, essays*. UK: Bogle L'Ouverture Publications.

———. (1991). *Papa Moose's nursery rhymes*. Goa: The Other India Press.

———. (1992). *Zerbrochene traume*. Germany: Horlemann Press.

———. (1994). *Broken buds*. Goa: The Other India Press

———. (1999). *Shrapnel silence & sand*. UK: Bogle L'Ouverture Publications.

———. (2000). *Rags & ragas*. Nepal: Taraghale Publictions.

———.(n.d.) Literature and human rights — the poet as "the equaliser" in the 21st century. Washington: Omni Shore Hotel. Talk presented at Washington Times Foundation.

Secondary Texts

Addison, K. (1982, December 5). Cecil Rajendara: A third world poet and his works. *Bangkok Post,* (n.p.)

Face to face with Cecil Rajendra. (1996, Summer). *Focus*. (pp.30–32.)

Pereira, A. (1997). Cecil Rajendra: Rebel with a cause. *His*. February

Taylor, C. (1979, December 28). Looking at the darker side. *Asiaweek* (Literary supplement), (n.p).

Wong, P. N. (1992, March 4). Poet betrayed by his own words. *New Straits Times*, (n.p)

Hilary Tham

6.0 Epigraph

> . . . my aims have grown—I write to lead an examined life, to not simply exist without thought. I also write to celebrate life, the wonder of people, and nature and the miracle of being alive. I write to preserve my cultural heritage, to pass it on to my children and future generations; I hope my poems become bridges of understanding between peoples for we are all sisters and brothers under the skin. To make connections—in hopes that a reader somewhere, sometime, will feel less alone in reading one of my poems . . .
>
> — Hilary Tham, *Lane with No Name*
> (1997, p. 203)

6.1   Introduction

Hilary Tham Choy Kam was born on August 20, 1946 in Klang, the royal town of Selangor. She was sent to Kelang Convent School for primary and secondary education. From 1964 to 1966, she did two years of secondary education (Lower and Upper Six) at St John's Institution on Bukit Nanas in Kuala Lumpur. From 1967 to 1970, she majored in English Literature at University of Malaya. In 1971, she married a Jewish American, Joseph Ray Goldberg, and left Malaysia. Tham now adopts the Jewish faith, and has three daughters. A prolific writer, Tham has published about six anthologies of poetry, a number of short stories and a memoir. *No Gods Today* was published in Malaysia in 1969 but other anthologies that followed were all published in the United States of America. Her American works will be considered because many of them evoke the poet's Malaysian memories.

Tham's memoir of her Malaysian-Chinese girlhood entitled

Lane with No Name is a sincere and moving account of her Malaysian chapter. While one is mindful of selective memory in the writing of autobiographic texts, Tham's memoir provides an insightful account of her childhood and growing up years. When read together with Tham's poetry, the memoir offers glimpses into her private life.

Born the second child and eldest daughter in a family of six, the Tham family was surrounded by material poverty and anguish. Her parents had an arranged marriage—while her father had several photographs of prospective brides to choose from, her mother had no choice when she was chosen to be the bride. Father Tham lived by the principle of "easy come, easy go", and it was Tham's mother, Au Lin Tei, the straightforward "iron-hand without velvet glove" autocrat (1997, p. 125), who was resourceful to make ends meet. Despite having to live with a very difficult mother-in-law, a womanising husband and losing a child, she had the vision of what she wanted her children to be. Due to her prudent character, she managed to buy a house for seven hundred dollars in a nameless lane along Meru Road in Klang. Despite the hardship, Tham's mother instilled a sense of purpose in her daughter's life. Living by Cantonese proverbs, she always had a proverb for any situation. Tham says:

> I often think that Cantonese proverbs are like bouillon cubes: they are always compact, evocative word pictures that pack a lot of meaning and punch.... Growing up as I did, with a language that was terse, concentrated, and full of rhymes and images, it was natural for me to think in metaphors and to turn to the reading and writing of poetry. My mother's favourite teaching proverb was this : "...Helping others, do your very best. Sending Buddha, escort him to the West." She insisted we should do any task we accepted responsibly and completely. She did not believe in feeling sorry for oneself or in crying over bad luck: "...The horse being dead, get down and

walk." She said that since we were too poor to have horses, or a car, well then, we could walk, we were lucky, we had two good legs. But she was wrong about our having no horses; she gave us strong horses named "Integrity", "Brave Heart", and "Taking Responsibility"; she gave us steady horses named "Clean as Water, Never Sticky with Debts", "Good Will" and "Wearing Eyes to See People", she gave us mountain-climbing horses named "Motivation" and "Respectfully Refusing to Quit". Endowed with such horses, I have never felt poor.

(1997, pp. 44–47)

Tham was greatly influenced by her mother's character. At thirteen, she became her mother's confidante, and became aware of the loneliness and suffering of the older woman:

I stopped admiring your father years ago. When Second Daughter died. When she was sick and he did not care enough to come home to take her to the doctor. It's hard to admire a selfish man who takes food from his children's mouths to take other women out to dinner. All these years, week in and week out, I am begging him for housekeeping money. Each time I beg, another piece of my heart turns to stone." . . .My mother explained that she could not abandon us children to the hardships a second wife would inflict on us; she could not earn enough to take us with her. Women who were dependent on their husbands had to shut their eyes (and mouths) to things like mistresses. My mother was progressive in her outlook. She believed fervently that times were changing. She was determined on equality for her daughters—we were to have as much education as we could attain. She knew daughters needed it more. She had sworn her daughters would not suffer as she had to.

(1997, pp. 119–120)

Tham's mother trained her children to be financially secured. Tham herself understood the pain of being powerless and caged, and thanked her mother "for the lessons she taught me, consciously and unconsciously" (1997, p. 21).

Other women whom Tham came across with in her life were also influential. Sister Louis at the Convent had vivacity, a lively way of speaking. So unlike her tired mother and difficult grandmother, Sister Louis brims over with life and energy and enthusiasm. As Tham ironically muses, "By contrast, all the wives and mothers I knew were tired, worn-out, often bad-tempered, generally unhappy women" (1997, p. 93).

Another female figure, a grandmother of an expatriate friend, provides another model of a charming elderly woman. Tham says, "Nana amazed me, delighted me, constantly. She was so different from the grandmothers I knew. I had thought grandmothers soured in old age. They always wore somber colours and disapproved of laughter and young people. Nana showed me that old age was what you made of it" (1997, p. 139).

Memories of a sister who died at the age of three left deep scars in Tham's memories. Tham says:

> Later, I learned that the souls of deceased male children were given a place in the ancestral tablet on the family altar and received part of descendants' offerings. And that the souls of deceased unmarried daughters were left out in the cold, due to the Chinese practice of patrilineal descent. Only when a girl is married does she acquire a rightful place in her husband's ancestral tablet, especially if she produces male offspring. It angered me that my sister was not included in our family tablet because she had been born a girl. And died before marriage.
>
> (1997, p. 87)

Her writing life took on a positive note at high school. Brother Celestine, her English teacher in Form Six took delight in her early poems. She was also an avid reader—indiscriminately reading anything she could get her hands on, "Gone with the wind, Dracula, World fairy tales. She read Poe, Emily Dickinson, the Bronte sisters, Georgette Heyer, Jane Austen, George Eliot, Barbara Carland, Charles Dickens. She also extended her reading of Chinese literature—Lin Yutang, *The Three Kingdoms, Dream of the Red Chamber* (1997, p. 30). Her English nuns at school provided the language and European culture so different from the Chinese one. Later on, at fifteen, she befriended a Eurasian, Susan L. who opened more doors for Tham. Tham wrote her first poem in jest. Using Wordsworth as a source, she wrote *Ode Upon Dennis Belly*. Everybody— Susan, Nana, and even Dennis liked it. Susan was Tham's literary circle—they discussed novels, poetry and drama. Therefore, even though there was little at home to nurture her literary talents, there was plenty of external driving force, which propelled Tham towards writing. Later on, it was the doctor to Susan's mother, who was also doctor to the Selangor Royal Family, who recommended Tham as a tutor to the princesses.

Reading Tham's *Lane with No Name* exposes reasons why Tham is preoccupied with women issues; her mother's tempestuous relationship with her husband, the unpredictable behaviour of her grandmother, the general condition of Chinese women around her provided one scenario of women. The English nuns, her Eurasian friend Susan, Mrs. L and Nana, and the English characters in the fiction she read provided another scenario. Tham's works, both short stories and poetry, and her memoir, show a preoccupation with the issues of being a woman, especially a Chinese one.

6.2   Discussion of works

Tham is known as a poet but she has also written short stories: *The Discovery* (1967), *The Unclean* (1967) and *Unborn Tomorrow* (1967). *The Discovery*, for example, illustrates her criticism of men and their philandering ways. Kim San discovers that his father, whom he idolises, is a womaniser. Initially he blames his mother for her addiction to mahjong, which drives his father to the arms of other women, but he realises that his father is also to be blamed for the dysfunctional family. He vows to be a faithful husband. At the close of the story, however, Kim San's wife and her friends settle down for a mahjong session, and his son comments that "daddy is away on a business trip," an excuse reminiscent of Kim San's own father's excuse for staying away from home. Having read the memoir, this story takes on a darker aspect because Tham has first hand experience of what it feels like to have an absent and womanising father.

In *Unborn Tomorrow*, Tham explores the insubordination of Chinese women. In her memoir, Tham reminisces her grandmother's partial treatment to the males in the family:

> My paternal grandmother made no effort to disguise her partiality for the boys in the family. Elder Brother was given an egg for breakfast. She'd heap meat (whenever we had it) on his rice. Because he was the boy.

(1997, p. 28)

Being in the Chinese culture constricts her role as a woman:

> I admit I was guilty of male envy—I wanted the freedom that our society gave men, but not women. The freedom to be fully themselves, not compressed, squeezed tightly into molds, like the bound feet of my grandmother's generation. I felt constricted. I wanted to learn what sort of person I could be, if free to explore all the interesting paths marked "not for women", "not for sensible Chinese who must focus on earning money and giving their parents grandchildren and filial piety". I wanted to be free to do and think and be. And I wanted to write about all the process, the discovery, the being alive. . . "

(1997, p. 202)

Many things about Chinese culture, which oppress women become Tham's subject matter in her works. In her memoir she writes that:

> I hated the physical process of becoming a woman. Month after month, I had "accidents" that mortified me, embarrassed me. It was made worse by the fact there would be no end to this process for the next forty years, an eternity to a teenager. At that time, a newspaper article brought me comfort. In Sweden, the first sex-change operations had been performed successfully. Though they were to change men into women, I felt cheered and confident that Western medicine would have achieved the ability to do the opposite operation by the time I grew up and saved enough money. I resolved to have my sex changed."
>
> (1997, p. 115)

Although she did not have a sex-operation, the female voice in her works champions the rights of women. For example, her short story the *Unborn Tomorrow* tells the tragic death of a girl because she dies of drowning. While her brother has been given swimming lessons, she misses out because of her sex. At the picnic, her brother promises to teach her but she dies at the outing. Chooi King's diary describes the sexual discrimination:

> ...I wish I were a boy—it's much more fun . . . Chee King can go out and play games in school and join the scouts, And I cannot. Just because I am a girl, I must wear skirts and walk nicely and sit properly and must not shout or climb trees or fly kites, like Chee King does. IT'S NOT FAIR! I want to enjoy myself...
>
> (1967, p. 40)

The protagonist yearns to break the confines of traditions. When she dies of drowning, the irony of living up to traditions which subordinate women, is obvious.

Edwin Thumboo's *The Second Tongue* includes eight of Tham's poems. The poems relate to a variety of issues: place and time, growing up, moods and persons, *kampung* and town. Tham's use of nature is prevalent in these poems and she exploits it as a metaphor for life and people. For example, in her poem *Sitting in Grass*, Tham highlights the similarity between the growing young woman and the occurrence of the beetle climbing up a *lalang* leaf. The speaker sees a parallel between the hair on her arms and the hair on the *lalang*. Just as she furtively and silently matures into a woman, so is the movement of the beetle.

Nor Faridah and Quayum (2000) notice echoes of Wordsworth's *Daffodils* and Whitman's *I Sing the Body Electric* in *Sitting in Grass* (p. 123). However, one is struck by a closer connection to Blakes' poems of experience. When the speaker says, "And as I touch the skin on my thighs/Young as the petal of a rose", a connection with Blake's *Sick Rose* comes to mind. While in the *Sick Rose* the male speaker berates the woman's loss of innocence and sexual stirrings, here the female speaker celebrates her sexuality. In an interview, Tham says that the women's movement that started in the 1960s definitely influenced her celebration of the female body. She says, "I wrote *Sitting in Grass* in a moment of discovery of self, and I liked the poem then and today still, as a protest against the taboo against self-examination, the unspoken social rule that women should not be proud of, or take pride in, their bodies feeling alive. I had a lump in my breast and, when I saw a doctor about it, I remember my appalled embarrassment and indignant denial when she asked me if I examined my breasts often. The idea of touching one's own body was taboo in the 1960s. Now, women know it is false modesty..." (1997, p. 206).

In another poem, *Grass* Tham extends the nature imagery to highlight the contrast between escapism and reality. In the poem, the speaker speaks to an addressee, "Tell me, have you watched the grass grow?" The speaker, like the addressee, often takes flight to the "green patch", and takes comfort watching nature at work—the grass blade arching "its slender wand", the sound of grass "slither[ing]". These simple workings of nature act momentarily to deaden worldly pains. But as the speaker warns, even the grass looks grotesque at night because when one wakes up from her reverie, she returns to the present world where pain exists, and she must learn to deal with it.

Tham's early poems also show a preoccupation with her aims in life. From her memoir, one can discern a stubborn determination to move forward. In *Vocation*, the speaker claims that she has "put away the toys of [her] youth and risen to the taunting of the crow"(1969, p.14). Living in Klang where crows abound, Tham again looks to nature to see its similarity with the situation of the speaker. Crows flock together and guard their kind fiercely, but the speaker is about to sever her roots—"Tomorrow I shall take down my icons from the wall/Sweep not the settled dust of accumulated years;/Leave not a memory nor an echo" (1969, p. 29). Again, Tham's memoir provides a possible meaning. Tham, having married her American husband, has to leave Malaysia—her parents, siblings, friends to start a new life. She says in the memoir:

> The tall, uniformed customs officer . . . had been friendly. "Welcome to America. Anything to declare?" …"No, nothing to declare," Joe answered for us. Nothing except guilt, my mind said silently. In following my heart, I had left my family and abandoned my family obligations."
>
> (1997, p. 2)

The final two lines of her sonnet "The dead cannot bury themselves; the living must,/Or be buried by the putrefying remains" imply that she cannot completely abandon her roots because she will be forever haunted by guilt which can be as grim as the remains of corpses.

In her early works, Tham imitates closely the structure of standard English, probably because her audience consists of native speakers (Brother Celestine, Susan and her family). Although the sentiments she conveys have local flavour, the language is insipid. Her later poems show a more colourful rendering of the diasporic, older writer. For example, the poem *That You Are What They Say* shows Tham being selective with her words and yet they are not as memorable as her later poem where she takes care with the way in which she arranges her words:

> That you are what you say
> I cannot accept
>   and yet —
> That statement, like yeast-grain,
>   ferments and foments
>   pushing out my sanity
> Till my mind is one protest,
>   and I am dark and dire;
>   heavy in my hands
>   a coil of disgust

(1969, p. 18)

Like many other Malaysian poets of her time, with no tradition to call their own, they copied the structure of English. Tham says that she "was intoxicated with alliteration and big polysyllabic words, scattering them through [her] poems like a child showing off" (1997, p. 94). Hence, Tham's poems show a conscious effort to find words, which alliterate, making them a little choppy. Her later poems, however, flow wonderfully that one could read them over and over again, each time the senses are affected in a higher degree.

Certain nouns are specifically Malay, for example, *lalang*—the kind of grass whose blades are so sharp they can cut the undiscerning trespasser quite easily. The *lalang* evoked here suggests a Malaysian wild landscape; it also shows the similarity of the wilderness of the fauna with the growth of the young woman. In *Vocation*, Tham brings in a landscape familiar to her—the crows. She says: "I have put away the toys of my youth and

110

risen to the taunting of the crow". From a scientific point of view, crows are among the most intelligent and adaptable of birds. Even in the breeding season, crows gather to mob owls and other predators. Crows, in turn may be mobbed by other birds, because their omnivorous diet includes eggs and nestlings as well as other small animals, vegetable matter, carrion and garbage. In some agricultural areas, crows are considered great pests, which accounts for the invention of the scarecrow. The young are cared for by both parents. The voices of crows are loud and usually harsh.

The use of crows as a metaphor highlights the narrator's position as someone torn between two worlds. The harsh and loud call for filial gratitude runs contrary to the call of romantic love, of wanting to break ties with family, culture and religion. But as one is reminded of the crows' resourcefulness and adaptability, one is also certain that the narrator will adapt to her new circumstances.

Life in the United States gave Tham the edge in her writing. While her poems produced in Malaysia had depth, it is her American-produced poems which show maturity as a poet. Most of her poems, though, reveal her links with Malaysia and her Malaysian upbringing. In the *Paper Boats* anthology, the poems could be read as autobiographical. *The Arranged Marriage* describes the relationship between the speaker's father and mother, reminiscent of the stories in her memoir:

> Mother no longer laughed at his stories.
> She saw him through a fret of unpaid
> Landlords, gonorrhea afflictions,
> Five needy children, the pain
>
> Of a sixth child dying.
> They wept when Sister died. Separately.

(1987,p. 3)

The speaker speaks honestly of her father's weaknesses while paying tribute to her mother who has to work doubly hard to make up for her husband's ways. It is this mother's characteristics that Tham admired, that became the catalyst for her "Mrs. Wei's" poems.

"Mrs Wei's" poems are poems full of humour about a personality called Mrs Wei who has her own way of seeing the world. Whether Mrs Wei is in the East or West, her attitude towards the things she sees is always honest and simple, but it strikes a chord in all of us. For example, Mrs Wei, upon learning that a monk has tried to touch a young girl on the bus, goes up to the man of religion and reprimands him:

> Mrs Wei rose in wrath, hissed to the girl
> To watch her bags and began to bellow.
> "Lecher! Animal! Reptile in saffron robe!
>
> Secret Eater of Forbidden Meat!
> Molesting young girls on buses!
> I'll report you to your Abbot,
>
> You vomit on Buddha's face!"
> Eyes turned. Heads turned. In silence,
> He took the path that opened to the exit.

(1987, p. 58)

Mrs Wei then advises the young girl to carry a safety pin so that "when a scum like that / surfaces, stab it in the ass" (1987, p. 58). Not afraid to speak up, standing up for one's rights, superstitious but at the same time, commonsensical, Mrs Wei is a typical Chinese mother who surfaces so often in Tham's poems.

Tham's American poems also reveal the contrast between practices of the East and West. In *Ancestor Worship*, for example, the Western and Eastern practices of respecting the dead is given a new perspective. While an Englishman puts flowers on his mother's grave, a Chinese woman spreads "a feast of roast chicken, *mu shu* pork, noodles" before her father's grave. When asked by the Englishman when is her father coming out to eat the food, the woman smilingly answered, "[At the] same time your mother come[s] to smell [the] flowers" (1994, p. 45). Here Tham shows the Chinese practice of respecting the dead is as legitimate as the Western more "genteel" way. By giving the Chinese woman the last say, Tham is poking fun at the Englishman as he tries to belittle the Chinese customs.

6.3 Conclusion

Other poems speak of her American Jewish life, often making links with her children's, husband's and friends' lives. When read against the memoir, most of her poems can be traced to her concerns about her immediate family members and friends. Tham remembers Malaysia, and everything about it with fond memories; these provide her impetus for her writings. Tham's voice is not singularly Malaysian; her many worlds—Chinese, Jewish, Malaysian and American—have all contributed to making her complex tapestry of poetry.

Bibliography

Tham, H. (1967). *LIDRA: Journal of the Literary and Dramatic Association of Malaya*, 6, (pp. 41–44).

——. (1967). The discovery. *Paper boats: An anthology of Malaysian creative writing*, 1, (pp.31–34).

——. (1969). *No gods today*. Kuala Lumpur: (n.p)

——. (1987, Spring). Picture bride. *Antietam Review*,(pp.1–4).

——. (1989). *Bad names for women*. Washington: The Word Works.

——.(1992). *Tigerbone Wine: Poems*. Washington: Three Continents Press.

———. (1993). *Paper boats: Poems of Hilary Tham*. (2nd ed.). Washington: Three Continents Press.

——. (1994). *Men and other strange myths: Poems and art*. Colorado: Three Continents Press.

——. (1997). *Lane with no name: Memoirs and poems of a Malaysian — Chinese girlhood*. Colorado: Lynne Rienner Publishers.

——. Unborn tomorrow. (1997) *The annual non-hostellite magazine, University Malaya*, (pp. 38–42).(Unpublished).

——. (2000). *Counting: A long poem*. Washington: The Word Works.

Lloyd Fernando

7.0 Epigraph

Nearly all of us, then, all over the world are united at least in facing the problems presented by different cultural norms co-existing, easily or uneasily, within the boundaries of our respective nations. We have to re-order, accept, or discard elements from a diverse array of beliefs, assumptions, modes of communication, customs and habits because, despite significant variations, we have become aware of the new dimension in development of cultures: the last fifty years have confirmed us all in a bicultural phase which had been building up for the previous three centuries. Cautiously, I advance this as a principle epitomising the underlying tension in everything we say and do nowadays. We search for unity, homogeneity, while being confronted by the reality of heterogeneity.

—Lloyd Fernando, *Cultures in Conflict*
(1986, p. 3)

7.1 Introduction

Lloyd Fernando was born in Sri Lanka on the May 31, 1926. He then followed his family to Singapore where he grew up and received his education. When his parents decided to return to Sri Lanka, the sixteen-year-old Fernando decided to stay behind. He continued to fund his education by taking odd jobs like working as a labourer, trishaw rider and an apprentice mechanic. He later took part time jobs as a radio broadcasting assistant and newsreader. He successfully graduated with double Honours degrees in English and Philosophy from the University of Singapore. As he says, the choice of majoring in philosophy was due to his need to find answers to the numerous questions he had at the time.

He later went on to acquire his Ph.D. from the University of Leeds. He began teaching at University of Malaya in 1967, and was the head of the English Department for a period. Whilst lecturing at the University, Fernando took up law purely by chance, and later decided to be a lawyer in order to not stop working upon reaching a retirement age, as he had two school going children at the time. In 1978, he left the academic profession to concentrate on his law profession.

He began writing at the age of fifteen. He describes writing as taking snapshots of the society and showing the reality without being sentimental. He credits, among others, Tolstoy, for influencing his appreciation for the significance of society in literature. He also acknowledges the influence of Aristotle's *Poetics* in forming the classical structure of his second novel *Green is the Colour*, for example in the inclusion of the exposition, rising action, climax and resolution. He was also an ardent reader of Joseph Conrad's works. He felt that Conrad, unlike many Caucasian writers of his time, attempted to be more "pro-people" (Lai & Goh, 1995) without being discriminatory of any one race.

Fernando approaches his writing in a very disciplined manner. He begins writing at eight in the morning, and only takes breaks for lunch and tea. He does describe it as inculcating a habit, which becomes sharpened with constant training. He takes the extra effort to travel both within and outside the country in search of personal experiences, which will form the seeds of his fiction. For his first novel, Fernando travelled around the peninsular; he went to Kelantan, Kedah and down south. For his second novel, he took a train ride to Singapore, as he says to push himself to consider the foundation of his story.

Fernando has a vast experience in the literary world and many different careers. A former English professor-cum-lawyer, he has been the editor of the literary journal *Tenggara* for eight years and edited two volumes of Malaysian short stories. He has written two novels—*Scorpion Orchid* (1976 &1991) and *Green is the Colour* (1993), and a collection of critical articles—*Cultures in Conflict*, and a short story *Surja Singh*. He has also written some radio scripts, and a play version of his first novel which won him the second prize at the 1993 *NST*-Esso playwriting competition [The play was recently published in Mohammad A. Quayum's *Anthology of Malaysian Literature in English* (2003)].

Even though his novels are based on the Malayan/Malaysian experience, his target audience include people of South East Asia. In doing so, he accepts the possibility that he will exclude other readerships, especially the western audience. However, the writer-critic holds to the belief that he has to be true to his identity and not abide by the expectations of others. As he says, "I write for us . . . I think it is very important because I try to shift the attention to show that life is interesting here" (Lai & Goh, 1995). At the core of his fiction is a good old storyline that people can identify with.

Fernando is one of the few Malaysian writers who attempts to bridge the ethnic divide by creating fiction which contains a community of multicultural characters who all have a significant part in the story line. He admits that it is a task to represent communities, which one is not familiar with. However, he says that it is not impossible as one merely needs "to look harder, think harder and empathise much more" (*NST*, March 18, 1992, n.p).

Fernando's fiction highlights innovative styles and techniques of prose writing stretching the readers' ability to respond and relate, especially fellow Malaysians. He realises that such an approach could create problems both to new and old readers. However, as he stresses, an approach has to be done in order to achieve his intended literary objective:

> I knew I would be taxing both new and old readers alike with the themes I chose, the people I created, the manner in which I told my story, the issues I brought up and the language I used. I wanted to correct an imbalance

towards Western viewpoints that we in our part of the world have lived with for centuries.

(*NST*, December 12, 1997, n.p)

The need to re-represent the Malayan/Malaysian history and celebrate a "local" viewpoint is synonymous to both his fiction and critical articles. As critics like M. E. Vethamani commented, Fernando has stayed "true to his call as a literary critic for Malaysian writers to resort to local myths and history" (*Wasafiri*, 21, p. 52). At a time when his fellow compatriots were complaining about the lack of a literary tradition for Malaysian writing in English to emulate, Fernando set the pace by tapping into the available resources within the nation's heritage and history as his platform to weave his fiction.

7.2   Discussion of works

This section discusses Fernando's fictions, in particular the techniques and concerns in his novels which many critics have stated as an identifiable new approach to a Malaysian literary tradition. His first novel, *Scorpion Orchid* presents the story of four university friends of different ethnic background: Sabran, a Malay; Santinathan, an Indian; Guan Kheng, a Chinese; and Peter, a Eurasian. The friendship between these four young men is challenged with the political and social changes that take place in Singapore during the pre-independence stage. As the political climate whips into frenzy, the relationship between the four is tested to the limits. Social niceties are stripped away as the characters are reduced to the bare bones of their racial prejudices. Their self-absorbed passion for individual survival in the face of racial upheaval leads them to expose their bloodiest thoughts, and strike out in sheer self-preservation. Abdul Majid Baksh (1981) suggests that Fernando's first novel is also "the first Malaysian novel in English to take a hard look at the realities of the Malaysian situation, and to consider in a forthright manner the inexpressible and perhaps, even inexplicable racial dilemma confronting the country and to try and suggest not only a solution to the racial problem but also a perspective or approach to it" (p. 52).

His second novel, *Green is the Colour* is a story about four individuals—Sara, Yun Ming, Dahlan and Gita, again of different racial/cultural background brought together through friendship or mutual acquaintance after the bloody May 1969 riots. Like *Scorpion Orchid*, the characters of Fernando's second novel continue to struggle with internal and external conflicts towards meeting personal needs and public expectations given the pluralistic landscape of the newly independent nation. As Quayum (2001) suggests, Fernando's *Green is the Colour* poses this central question: "How can Malaysia with its plurality and multiplicity find unity?" (p. 168).

The third instalment to Fernando's prose is his short story *Surja Singh*, the story of a 28-year-old soldier who lives through the Japanese Occupation and later, the return of the British. It is a story about loyalty and sense of belonging or as reviewed in *The Statesmen* (2002), it is a story of "guilt and dislocation".

Fernando's fiction is a marriage of his creative energy with his critical thoughts on what makes a good literary tradition for Malaysian fiction. To begin with, he gave both novels specific historical settings. *Scorpion Orchid* is set in colonial Singapore, specific during British colonisation in the 1950s while *Green is the Colour* is set in post-May 1969 Malaysia. Utilising the historical settings, Fernando takes contemporary readers back in time and presents a different landscape than the one they perhaps are familiar with. Such a technique of "interfaced histories" as Roxas-Tope (1998) states, "reminds the readers that what may seem current has already occurred in the past" (p. 141). In addition, by setting the events in the past the author gives clarity to issues that had unfolded at a specific point in time, i.e. "to open history to the non-linear reading"(*ibid.*). As he says, "if you set it in a contemporary period, you cannot separate the important from the ephemeral... lots of trivia get in. *Scorpion Orchid* is about people and how events of that time affected them" (*NST*, March 18, 1992, p. 33).

In addition to historical settings, Fernando's novels also enjoy other trappings in the form of literary traditions. In *Scorpion Orchid*, Fernando experimented with bridging two literary traditions—the ones in Malay and in English, by incorporating extracts from classical Malay literatures including *Hikayat Abdullah, Sejarah Melayu* and *Hikayat Hang Tuah*, in weaving his fiction. *Green is the Colour*, on the other hand, is an allusion to the 18th century Malay classic *Misa Melayu*, as the note at the end of the novel states, "The writing of this novel was suggested by an episode in *Misa Melayu*." Critics have suggested that such incorporations show-cases the author's need to move away from a Eurocentric representation of the nation to one "more consonant with the local's experience and sense of a usurped history" (Koh, 2001, p. 163).

Through the incorporations of history and classical literatures, Fernando presents a possible local literary tradition of Malaysian literature in English that Malaysians could emulate. As he states, these techniques might alienate certain readers, local and foreign alike. However ultimately, the creative power is heightened allowing for more versatility in literary style and utilisation of the English language, which are the writer's main aim:

> I have not minded that my approach may be alien to Western readers, including some of my own compatriots who have absorbed only Western habits of reading English. But it did lead me to a care for style in language, which was as much travail as excitement.
>
> (*NST*, December 12, 1997, n.p)

Fernando is concerned with the issues pertaining to the nation as a whole without singling out any particular ethnic group. His concern with the position taken by the different characters is a close resemblance of the numerous voices in the country. He does not seek to represent any one community at the expense of another. The communal centred and self-centred characters have an equal footing in Fernando's fictions. Characters like Panglima and Omar from *Green is the Colour* are known for their "excessiveness" (Quayum, 2001, p. 170) in seeking to fulfil their self-interest at the expense of others including their loved one. While Sara and Yun Ming try to keep a balance between fulfilling their self-interest and meeting the demands of the community and nation.

Fernando also allows his characters to be of different mindsets—both conservative and modern, in order to highlight the tensions that can be seen when the two extremes meet. In addition, the sense of modernity in the character does not have to be a direct influence of Western education per se. In fact, he allows the opportunity for readers to question the verities in both Western and Eastern lifestyles. One character who tries to maintain balance between these two worlds is Sara's father, Lebai Hanafiah, who Quayum suggests is the "true humanitarian" (Quayum, 2001, p. 171) in the novel. As the Lebai states in *Green is the Colour*:

> [T]here are so many who want to force you to follow the right path. Each one's right path is the only one. I am tired of seeing the folly spread in the name of such right paths. I fear those who seek to come between me and love for all humanity. They are the source of hate and destruction.
>
> (1993, p. 116)

Lebai takes a more balanced approach to the issue of pluralism, especially in his ability to accept and tolerate the difference between his sense of faith and the one practised by another community. Perhaps, Fernando can be read as using the voice of his character to relay his own views about the issue of tolerance and acceptance of the "Other".

On the issue of racialised representation, the major ethnic groups in the country, namely the Malays, Chinese and Indians are given equal attention in Fernando's novels. As M. E. Vethamani states, "Fernando portray characters from different races in Malaysia and does not give any special attention to the Malaysian Indian" (*Wasafiri, 21*, p. 52). Stylistically, he uses individuals to represent not just a possible single voice in the community but as a possible representation of the group at large. Fernando also creates situations in his novels to allow opportunities for inter-race relations to take place, at all levels of the society and all levels of relationship—professional and personal. Consider the following interracial relationship Dahlan-Gita, Yun Ming-Sara, Panglima-Yun Ming (in *Green is the Colour*), Sabran-Peter-Santi-Guan Kheng, Sally-Peter, Sally-Santi, Sally-Guan Kheng, and Sally–Sabran (in *Scorpion Orchid*).

The thematic concerns of Fernando's fiction can be read in the writer's description of the Malaysian landscape:

> I feel Malaysians are now getting to know each other without the colonial set-up. People often say that in the old days, Ali, Ah Kow and Muthu lived happily together. It isn't a true picture
>
> In the past, we didn't have to rule the country and make certain decision. We just went out for our *teh tarik* and went home. It's a different exercise now… the rules of the game have changed. We're taking real stock of each other and have to adapt and adjust to each other. That's the first step towards real understanding.
>
> (*NST*, March 18, 1992. n.p)

It is the element of "adaptation and adjustment" that is the recurrent theme in his fictions. The various communities and individuals in Fernando's fictions are shown to constantly seek out their understanding of their sense of identity and sense of belonging, both to their community or ethnic group and to the land they now live in. Fernando challenges the quest for a national identity in a country filled with heterogeneity in terms of culture, religious and language. As Peter in *Scorpion Orchid* states towards the end of the novel:

I was born in Malacca speaking Portuguese. That's
because the Portuguese colonised us so many hundred
years ago. The Dutch didn't stay long enough . . . Then
because the British had ousted the Dutch, I learnt English
and forgot my Portuguese. It was like taking out the parts
and organs of my body and replacing them with others.
Then the Japs came and we were told to forget English,
learn Japanese . . . unlearning my language and learning
another. Now it seems I must unlearn it once more and
learn Malay.

(1976, p. 143)

Peter's frustration of the language issue is very pertinent to
the context of a multicultural setting like Malaysia. Language is a
tool to communicate as well as to unite people of disparate existence.
The language, which is also seen as "a bearer of the [cultural] values"
(Roxas-Tope, 1998, p. 76), provides the identification of one's sense
of belonging to a given land or community. Like the Eurasian Peter,
the other characters are faced with similar conflicts, torn between
adapting to the changes in the society and policies of the times and
hanging on to the given values of one's culture/community. Do
you continue to find points of attachment to the motherland be it
China or India, or do you make a drastic step to sever every tie and
begin to redefine your identity to the expectations and demands of
the new land? The tension between the two strong forces is at the
core of both novels. A possible outcome can be read in the words of
Yun Ming (in *Green is the Colour*), the would be nationalist of Chinese
ancestry, "Yun Ming found himself saying with fervour that the
Chinese and Indians had to forget where they came from. They must
follow one way of life, have one way of doing things. He caught
himself in time before being swept into saying they should have
one religion" (1993, p. 21).

On the aspect of narrative techniques, Fernando presents his
stories, as he admits (see introduction) using the classical structure

of fiction. It begins with the expositions of the issues faced by each character, both at personal and public levels, followed by the rising actions and revelations of conflicts, both internal and external, and later the climax and soon after, the denouement which ends the story. Having said that however, Fernando's fiction does not end on an idealistic note of "Edenic" possibilities in a multicultural nation. In fact, both novels leave the reader questioning the future of the nation given the true atmosphere of a pluralistic existence. The four university friends in *Scorpion Orchid* are shown to go their separate ways and the multiracial relationships especially between a Malay and non-Malay face tremendous reservations.

On the issue of characterisation, Fernando's characters are a community of dynamic and static personalities. Static characters are useful as catalysts for conflicts. The dynamic characters raise awareness of the possibilities of improvement in society—these characters initially create conflict for society but later become the instigators for reformation by changing their old ways. This way the writer does not come across as being too didactic with the pursuit of raising socio-political awareness. Stock characters that represent overt mindset towards creating the conflict in the story, like Panglima (in *Green is the Colour*) is a self-centred, materialistic, authority figure who uses the cause of the people to gain self-fulfillment.

Dynamic characters on the other hand, through their developments in the story present the issues raised in the novels. For example, Dahlan (in *Green is the Colour*) starts of being very radical and individualistic in his approach to fight the authority. However, extreme egalitarianism cannot function either. Throughout the course of the story, Dahlan constantly re-evaluates his own position, and begins to change his approach to the societal issues. Another character is Omar (in *Green is the Colour*) who approaches his life with an extremism of religious conviction due to external influences, at the expense of his marriage and friendship with those who are not of his faith but gradually realises that he had been misled. Yet the changes in Omar are too abrupt so much so that critics have considered it somewhat unrealistic.

With regards to representation of women, Fernando is obviously very conscious of his position. He admits to putting female characters at the centre of his novels partly because of his own academic research at the Ph.D. level, and partly because he has great sympathies for the "lousy deal" women have been getting in the world (Lai & Goh, 1995). In *Scorpion Orchid*, Sally or Salmah is befriended by the four friends. She becomes the main point of reference for them, not unlike the nation to which they belong. Critics have suggested that Sally is in fact a symbolic representation of the nation; one who is without any strong ethnic attachment is yet able to relate to everyone (Baksh, 1981, p. 53). In *Green is the Colour*, on the other hand, Siti Sara is torn between living by the stands of the community, and in particular her husband on the one hand, and living by her own needs, on another. Her "spirit of love and individualism" (Quayum, 2001, p. 171) creates one of the central conflicts in the story. She is shown to exercise her sense of agency, as the story ends, by deciding to leave Omar and telling him so.

Fernando also uses mystical/abstract characters to add to the complexity of the Malaysian landscape. Tok Said in *Scorpion Orchid* is, as critics have commented, a symbolic and enigmatic figure. He is considered as the "embodiment of the Malaysian consciousness, a psychological entity... in short, the country's consciousness" (Baksh, 1981, pp. 54–55). Through the incorporation of Tok Said, the writer has managed to personify the nation a step further. By giving Sally the social characteristics of the nation, i.e. not forming attachment to any ethnic group and by making Tok Said ever present in various parts of the nation, indirectly projecting the "voice of nationhood" (Subramaniam, 1996, p. 359), Fernando is finally able to give life to the nation in ways most Malaysian writers have not succeeded. As fellow writer-critic, K. S. Maniam says of Tok Said and Sally–Salmah, "the former represents the spiritual centre, the latter the more earthly centre of love" (2001, p. 82).

7.3 Conclusion

Lloyd Fernando's contribution to Malaysian literature in English is twofold. Like most writers of his generation, Fernando not only contributed to the creative corpus of the literature in English in the country, but he also serves as a vocal and thoughtful critic, raising issues and questions he feels crucial to the continuity and survival of Malaysian literature in English.

One such issue that has been debated for over decades is the usage of the English language to address the Malaysian. Malaysian writers in English have had to argue vehemently against accusations of imperialistic gestures due to their choice of language. In turn, these established writers feel they have been subject to marginalisation by the authority and the public (See discussions on Ee Tiang Hong, Wong Phui Nam and Kee Thuan Chye). Fernando's answer to the question "Why English?" is simply "this is the medium in which I am most skilled" (*NST*, December 10, 1997, n.p). Even though his native tongue is Sinhala, as a former professor of University of Malaya admits, it is his "original long-forgotten native tongue" (*ibid.*).

Fernando's notable approach in discussing issues pertaining to Malaysian literary scenes, such as the need to exercise greater flexibility as well as tolerance within a multicultural setting such as Malaysia, makes him a truly conscientious writer-critic. He constantly positions his thoughts and creative powers within multiracial parameters, which he feels is crucial in order to succeed. He appeals to his fellow Malaysian writers not to eliminate any community in their quest to write, stating, "What matters for him [the Malaysian writer in English] is that he writes about the heart, spirit and life in our part of the world, not just about one community, but about us all" (*ibid.*).

As a writer, Fernando puts into practice the issues he brings up as a literary critic. By incorporating the tradition, heritage and history of this country Fernando has paved the way for the creation of a literary tradition for Malaysian literature in English, one which is not based on the former imperial centre but on the resources within Malaysia.

Bibliography

Primary Texts

Fernando, L. (1968). *Twenty-two Malaysian stories*. London: Heinemann.

———. (1972). *New drama one*. London: Oxford University Press.

———. (1972). *New drama two*. London: Oxford University Press.

———. (1982). *Modern malaysian stories*. London: Heinemann.

———. (1986). *Cultures in conflict*. Singapore: Graham Brash.

———. (1992). *Scorpion orchid*. Singapore, Kuala Lumpur: Times Books. (Original work published 1976).

———. (1993). *Green is the Colour*. Singapore: Landmark Books Pte Ltd.

———. (1999). Surgah Singh. In D. Mukherjee, K. Singh and M. A. Quayum (eds.), *Merlion and the Hibiscus* (2002). London: Penguin Books.

———. (2000). Fell Sergeant in *Kunapipi, XXII*(1), (n.p)

———. (2003). Scorpion Orchid [play]. In M. A. Quayum (ed.), *Petals of Hibiscus. A representative anthology of Malaysian Literature in English* (pp.190–238). Petaling Jaya: Pearson Longman .

———. (1997, December, 10). Take on a world with language. *New Straits Times*, (n.p).

Secondary Texts

Baksh, A. M. (1981, December).The Malaysian racial dilemma in Lloyd Fernando's scorpion orchid. *SARE 3*, (pp.54–55).

Subramaniam, G. (1996). Ethnocentricity in postcolonial Malaysian literary works: Extent of unity in diversity. In Fadillah Merican et al. (eds.). *A view of our own. Ethnocentric perspectives in literature* (pp. 355–363). Fakulti Pengajian Bahasa, UKM

Kee, T. C. (1993, September, 15). Seasoned writers win the top prizes. *New Straits Times*, (p. 33).

Koh, T. A . (2001). The empires' orphans: stayers and quitters. In M. A. Quayum & P. Wicks (eds.), *A Bend in the river & Scorpion orchid Malaysian literature in English: A critical reader* (n.p) Malaysia: Longman.

Lai, Y. M. & Goh, A. A. Unpublished interview with Lloyd Fernando on August 17, 1995 at Lloyd Fernando & Razak Advocates & Solicitors, Kuala Lumpur.

Malachi, V. E. (1995). Malaysian, Singaporean and Fijian writers of the Indian diaspora. *Wasafiri 21*, (pp. 52–53).

Maniam, K. S. (1988, 2001. The Malaysian novelist: detachment or spiritual transcendence? In M. A. Quayum & P. Wicks (eds.), *Malaysian literature in English: A critical reader* (n.p). Malaysia: Longman.

Quayum, M. A. (2001). Shaping a new national destiny with dialogic vision: Fernando's green is the colour. In M. A. Quayum & P. Wicks (eds.), *Malaysian Literature in English: A critical reader* (p. 171). Malaysia: Longman.

Raihanah Mohd Mydin & D'Cruz, V. (1999). Private/public use of Malaysian literature in English. In Proceedings of the International Conference on Teaching and Learning. November 24-25, 2000. *Strategising teaching and learning in the 21st century*, 2, (pp. 722–732).

Wilson, B. (1996). The legacy of colonialism: issues of identity in Lloyd Fernando's green is the colour. In Fadillah Merican *et al.* (eds.), *A view of our own: Ethnocentric perspectives in literature* (n.p). Fakulti Pengajian Bahasa, UKM

Wicks, P. (2002). Parametters of malaysian identity in the novels of Lloyd Fernando and K. S. Maniam. *Asian profile 30*(1), (pp. 27–35).

Wong, P. N. (March 18, 1992). In fear of the scorpion. *New Straits Times*.

Wong, S. K. (2001). Unveiling Malaysian modernity and ethnicity: Lloyd Fernando's green is the colour. In Maznah Mohamad & S. K. Wong (eds.), *Risking Malaysia: culture, politics and identity* (n.p). Bangi: Penerbit UKM

Zalina Mohd. Lazim. (1996). Emerging voices in *Scorpion Orchid*. In Fadillah Merican *et al.* (eds.), *A view of our own: Ethnocentric perspectives in literature* (n.p). Fakulti Pengajian Bahasa, UKM.

Muhammad Haji Salleh

8.0 Epigraph
Revision then, is renewal, the adjustment of perspective,
senses given their edges and language tasted in its more
profound salt.

— Muhammad Haji Salleh's
foreword in *Time and Its People*
(1978, n.p)

8.1 Introduction

Muhammad Haji Salleh was born in a small rubber plantation
village called Temerloh, which is close to Taiping, in 1942, during
the Japanese Occupation of Malaya. Soon after his birth, the family
moved to a small town south of Seberang Prai, where the father
opened a sundry shop. However, when the price of rubber fell, the
family moved again, this time to Bukit Mertajam. It was in Bukit
Mertajam that Muhammad received his early education, and from
there he went to Malay College Kuala Kangsar (MCKK), a
prestigious boarding school for the Malay boys of the time, for his
secondary education.

His constant relocation in search of knowledge, apparently,
did not stop there. He pursued his teacher-training certificate at
the Malayan Teachers' College in Brinsford Lodge, England, and
later obtained his Bachelor's degree from the University of Malaya
(then in Singapore). In 1970, he completed his Master's degree from
University of Malaya, Malaysia and three years later received his
Ph.D. from the University of Michigan on a comparative reading of
Malay and Indonesian poetry. Parallel to the constant migration in
pursue of education is his teaching experience. Muhammad has
taught in numerous institutions locally and the world over, from
United Kingdom and United States of America to Europe and parts

of Asia, including Japan, Indonesia and Singapore. In an interview, he was coined to be diasporic on two accounts, both within the nation and internationally.

In terms of his earliest encounter with literature, Muhammad, like his contemporary such as Edwin Thumboo, was predominantly exposed to the works of canonical writers like Shakespeare, T. S. Eliot and W. B. Yeats, both at the high school level and later, at the University of Malaya in Singapore. However, later on his encounter with Lloyd Fernando, another eminent Malaysian writer, who was then the Head of the English Department at University of Malaya, opened a new direction in his journey into literary territory. Fernando was experimenting with the inclusion of Malaysian and Southeast Asian literatures in the department, and his encouragement of the poet's own interest in the region's literary tradition, assisted Muhammad's literary scholarship to attain different heights. His graduate research took him to Indonesia where he uncovered newfound passion for the region's finest and best.

Muhammad's stay abroad, be that as a student or teacher or even researcher, over the years has deepened his sensibilities for and about international and regional writers such as Pablo Neruda, Chairil Anwar, Subagio Sastrowardojo and Baha Zain, to name but a few.

Muhammad's appreciation for literature stems from his ability to disregard overt differences in the literature's origin be it from Japan, India, Europe or Indonesia, and his capacity to embrace them as a source of wisdom. As a poet, he brings similar sensibilities into his writings, using personal experiences to speak of more universal themes. The impetus to stay creative is within him and writing poetry is primarily an act to fulfil himself. As he says, "You write for yourself as much as about your people" (Fadillah Merican, 2003, p. 16).

However, his writings have come under criticism by certain sections of the society for its nationalistic undercurrents, as they are seen to be too "communally-centred". In response, the poet subverts such criticism by repositioning himself on the self-community continuum citing that his poetry is both self- and community-centred, as he rightly states, "My poetry is 'communally-centred' in as much as I write about myself, a Malay and the community I know best, my own" (Fadillah Merican, 2003, p. 15).

His decision to stop writing creatively in English and concentrate purely in the production of Malay poetry also became a point of debate by critics who saw it as capitulating to nationalistic pressure. At a time when language and literature became a political issue, Muhammad was seen as caving in to the demands made by the authorities for Malaysians to use the National language instead of the "colonial tongue", English. Citing freedom and responsibility, his response on his choice of language is thus, "the metaphors do not come from England or Australia. They are taken from real life lived in Malaysia or Nusantara. But English is not a living language for me for I feel it is pretentious to live my life in English in Malaysia. And as a Malaysian I am responsible towards my mother tongue. I have stopped writing poetry in English now" (Fadillah Merican, 2003, p. 27).

8.2 Discussion of works

The bulk of the discussion on Muhammad's poetry for this chapter will be based on *Rowing Down Two Rivers*, his most recent reproduction of his earlier works. The poems are taken from the English translation of selected Malay poems in *Beyond the Archipelago* (1995) and his first anthology of English poems, *Time and Its People* (1978). The readings of his poetry will revolve around issues and concerns highlighted by critics over the years.

To begin with, in terms of genre, Muhammad's poetry can be categorised as lyric for their use of first person voice to express thoughts and feelings of the persona on a given subject. Such examples include "islanders", "among vegetables", "seeds", "on a journey" and many others including the following extract from the lyric aptly entitled "self portrait" in *Rowing Down Two Rivers*:

> for many days i died,
> killed by my own reflection,
> but immediately awakened
> with the sprinkle of life and blood
> children's call or the neighbour's invitation.
>
> i am a poet
> who must stand before the mirror
> and receive every sign.

(2000, p. 59)

The characteristics of his persona include aspects of humility and didacticism. His use of small caps throughout his poetry, especially the "i" have been read to connote humility, as Ruzy Suliza Hashim states, "certainly humbleness is one of them because many of Muhammad's poems show an "i" persona who is unassuming and self effacing" (Ruzy S. Hashim, 2003, p. 88).

However, other critics have suggested that Muhammad intentionally uses first person persona to allow greater reader participation, simultaneously making his writings a kind of didactic poetry. His persona, as Susanna Checketts (2003) suggests, functions as a teacher trying to create greater awareness in his readers on the issues affecting them. Such a reading of Muhammad's poetry does in fact put it within the parameter of Malay society where poets and writers do hold greater social responsibilities.

Imagery also plays an important role in Muhammad's writings, in particular the explicit inclusion of the local landscapes in the form of local fruits and vegetation. In *among vegetables* in *Rowing Down Two Rivers* (2000, p. 64), the persona paints the canvas of his thoughts with the colours of the local vegetation—the brown *kerdas*, the yellow ginger, the copper red sweet potato, the purple yam. While in the *forest's last day* the persona makes a plea for the gradual demise of the natural heritage as the "bloated lodger" brings down the "epic of the forest". Critics have suggested that his incorporation of aspects of the nature and land is the poet's way of finding identification to the nation.

The quotation in the prologue illustrates Muhammad Haji Salleh take on his poetry. This is a poet who revises his work of art, as he says in an interview, as many as ten times and keeps them for nearly two to three years to enable him to re-evaluate the poems with a sharper and more matured-eye. In addition, a reader of Muhammad's poetry will be quick to point out the appearance of certain recurrent motifs in his works over the years. These include the motif of the traveller who first appeared in the 1976 anthology selected by Edwin Thumboo in a poem entitled "the traveller", which later appeared in a different version in Muhammad's 1978 anthology *Time and Its People* as "traveller". Similar revising of other motif such as father, water or elements of water like rain and road, are also apparent in the various anthologies (See Bibliography for a comprehensive list).

His latest anthology *Rowing Down Two Rivers* (2000) in some ways is an exercise of refashioning some earlier poems. For example *homecoming* and *death like conception (for father)* have been revised in structure and content, and latter especially, is even given a new name as *as death, conception (for father)*. Similarly, the poem *blood* published in the 1976 collection of Singaporean and Malaysian poems selected by Edwin Thumboo was later revised and its last stanza dropped in both the 1978 publication *Time and its People* and the current book of poem *Rowing Down Two Rivers*.

Another element of revising of Muhammad's poetry appears in the exercise of the translation. As his later poems, post-1978 publication of *Time and Its People*, are originally written in Malay, his English poems in many ways are refashioning of the Malay ones, bringing his poetry to a larger audience. The translated poems do fit into the Malaysian Literature in English corpus, not simply for the fact that they are translated into English, but more so that the intended flavour and message of the original Malay is captured into English as the poet intends it.

As stated earlier, Muhammad's use of the recurrent motif of the traveller has become a trademark in his poetry. The traveller motif unsurprisingly becomes one of the central concerns of his writing. There are numerous verses that delve on the theme of the dual journey outwards and inwards. In the "straight bridge" in *Rowing Down Two Rivers* the persona speaks of peeling the layers of his "onion self" in each of the ten countries he has been to find himself:

> i peel my onion self
> to seek
> a young man on the bridge
> in ten countries—
> in each he stood
> pondering the river
> tributary of a firm continent.

(2000, p. 20)

However, it should also be stated that the elements of "the traveller" and "travelling" generally is not just a feature in the life of Muhammad's persona but equally true with the poet himself. In an interview, Muhammad acknowledges the need for travel as it provides him the seed of creativity towards answering questions about himself in particular in foreign settings. His approach to life, as a traveller in constant search of awareness and his ideology of living, his "frames of existence" as he calls it, is best captured in his words to his daughter, in the poem aptly titled *welcome home, juita* in the book *Rowing Down Two Rivers*. In this poem, the persona speaks of the need to be "free" in one's home in order to discover oneself and to allow one's ideas to find its form. However, the freedom, he realises is not in terms of attachment. Instead, its freedom to create which in fact is a kind of responsibility. The persona then proceeds to concretise freedom as into different imageries such as a chisel, colour and words, in order to create the allusion that this intangible yet all encompassing notion carries:

> freedom is the chisel in the master builder's hand
> colour to sight
> and words to thought.
> study its soul
> so that you may be free.

(2000, p. 36)

In the foreword to *Rowing Down Two Rivers* entitled "A Quid of Betel" (a translation of the Malay saying "*Sekapur Sirih*"), Muhammad pays homage to the innumerable places he has studied and taught literature and in turn created poetry. As he says, "Places help create poems, for to come to a place is to discover, to uproot and to change or experience change. Change gives the initial spark from which the brilliant literary lights are made" (2000, p. 11). Ironically, his journey outward, into foreign far away lands, became a journey of self discovery, as he adds, "The place may not be important... What is important is that they are a meaningful part of the life of the poet, which throws a light on what it means to be a human being" (2000, p. 14).

Similar themes of self-discovery can also be read in poems containing the motif of the road, which existed prominently in the *Time and Its People* anthology. The road, a universal symbol of the journey of life, presents the possibilities that Muhammad's persona face in his life. In *as death, conception (for father)*, the father's sudden death after a recovery is described as, "home is the last station/at the end of a truncated road" (2000, p. 14). In *going away*, the road again materialises as a symbol of the persona's life where people and places are mere distractions that one has to put up with:

> because we are travellers of sorts,
> places are only stops

along a road.
…
i collect faces
as i gather bits of love,
the fragmented justication
for a heap of experiences.
…
starting from a cross-road
and following intuition
we left a rendezvous
that a little time afforded.
now, I must go,
where the listless legs carry.

(2000, pp. 151–152)

Yet the encounters one faces along the journey of life is not always a distraction. In *to start anew*, they form the essence of the persona's sense of self which cannot be forgotten or left behind, unless one wishes to "grow old": "to go forward and forget / is to grow old, / to leave oneself behind, / carrying a luggage of ambivalence / for the foreign future" (2000, p. 158).

In addition to elements of travel, Muhammad's need to find a voice also colours his poetry. In *a heap of word*, the persona informs us of the world he creates in order to allow his voice to be heard:

once upon a time
as though fulfilling a vague promise
at an age tormented by the sense
i found a heap of words,
out of it I gathered
and built a world.
i sharpen its sound to my voice,
its sadness to the horse speech,
its laughter to the tragic.

(2000, p. 33)

The poet continues to experiment with issues and motifs in order to discover his voice. The search to uncover his voice in poetry also presents to the readers other thematic concerns including sense of displacement. Some of his poems describe the alienating effects the person feels in due to certain circumstances. For instance, in *this is no place for truth*, the persona identifies the alienating atmosphere he endures due the clash in attitudes between himself and the society, where the latter seems to live by corrupt and hypocritical practices:

> this is not the place for the naked word.
> if you entertain ambition,
> practise hiding your *keris* behind your back
> to stab when eyes turned away.
> make space for ceremonies,
> be diligent in fetching and sending your boss,
> arrange that you are always present at official receptions
> and often give him sweetmeats as offerings.
> and don't forget, caress his son's hair.
> before taking your leave ask him the price of his new car
> and how he polishes it.

(2000, p. 34)

Other poems like *world of debate, for kasturi* and *not mine* suggest a sense of detachment from his home soil created perhaps by a lack of acceptance. This brings in yet another important motif apparent in Muhammad's poetry, home.

Critics have suggested that as journey and travelling appear prominently, so does the quest for home. In his creative travelling, Muhammad's persona is in quest for the ideal space called home. In *the city is my home*, the persona accepts the lack of emotional attachment among the intellectually driven occupants of the city, yet as he says "this city is my home / the people my family" (2000, p. 154). In *returning for good*, on the other hand, critics have suggested that even though the persona admits to finding a sense of home, it is in fact a forced sense of belonging. The persona states that:

now standing on the newly repaired bund,
i learn to believe their belief.
now, as they call out to me
i wade the water
work till evening,
recognise the textures of earth,
tides of their feelings.
i know I am returning .
for good.

(2000, p. 198)

The persona in attempting to find a sense of connection with the *padi* farmers, surrendering to the same weathered life. Yet, can such a connection be considered a true sense of home or is it merely the abstracted notion of home?

The evolution of Muhammad's poetry post-1978 publication of *Time and Its People* took a more introspective approach to the issue of culture and tradition. His 1995 publication of *Beyond the Archipelago* utilised Malay classics as the point of departure in considering the concerns of the Malay community. Some of the poems, which have been republished in the current anthology *Rowing Down Two Rivers*, provide a revision of some prominent Malay classics like *Sejarah Melayu* and *Hikayat Hang Tuah* and folklore figures such as Si Tenggang. The inclusion of these classics contributes to the continuity of literary tradition linking modern Malaysian works to their forerunners.

8.3   Conclusion

Given Muhammad's strong stand on the need to explore the Malay literary scene, one could easily ask, where lies his contribution in the Malaysian Literature in English? Muhammad's decision to "abandon" writing in English is not unlike his African counterpart, Ngugi wa Thiong'o or James Ngugi, who due to the need to decolonise his mindset and contribute to the development of the

Kikuyu language and culture in Kenya, decided in 1977 to stop writing completely in English. Ngugi's primary argument is the inseparable link between language and culture, and how writing in English will dilute the particularities of the Kikuyu culture. Muhammad echoes similar arguments, as he says in an essay:

> As a young writer I was struggling to find myself, to strengthen my English poems with the Malaysian qualities as an attempt to give them a local identity. This seemed to be a conscious drive, for I was the only one with my background and was burdened with a task of marrying two cultures and languages. ...Though praised for being a poet in English, was I wrong to be known so, and abandoning Malay? Was I the Malaysian counterpart of ...Ngugi wa Thiongo...

(2001, n.p)

Muhammad's position though similar is not as complicated. He does continue to write in English, especially for literary scholarship and as stated at the beginning of the chapter, he translates selections of his Malay works, as he states in an interview, for his "non-Malay communities, non- Bahasa readership" (Fadillah Merican, 2003, p. 25).

The contribution Muhammad plays through the translation of his Malay poems is clear. A close reading between his translated Malay poems and his earlier English poems do reveal commonality in the themes of self-discovery and appreciation of the human existence. In a multicultural nation, voices from the various ethnic communities are needed to create a collage of the Malaysian Voice. Muhammad provides a distinct voice of the "cosmopolitan" (Raihanah Mohd Mydin & D'Cruz, 2003) Malay, in constant struggle to create an equilibrium between his more individuated side and the more communal one, who is rooted both in the western sensibilities of literary scholarship and the eastern, Malay, literary tradition. Even if they are translated versions of his Malay poems, they open an avenue into the mindset of the Malay community, especially in the discourse of literature in English. At a time when few Malays are venturing into serious English literature as opposed to the popular types, Muhammad's contribution cannot be sidelined.

Bibliography

Primary Texts

Muhammad Haji Salleh. (2000). *Rowing down two rivers*. Bangi: Penerbit UKM

————. (1995). *Beyond the archipelago*. Center for International Studies, Ohio University.

————. (1978). *Time and its people*. Kuala Lumpur: Heinemann Educational.

Thumboo, E. (1976). *The second tongue. An anthology of poetry from Malaysia and Singapore*. Singapore: Heinemann Educational Books (Asia) Ltd.

— contains 19 poems by Muhammad Haji Salleh (originally written in English), some of which appears in his later anthology *Time and its people*.

Muhammad Haji Salleh (ed.). (1978). *Selections from contemporary Malaysian poetry*. Kuala Lumpur: Penerbit Universiti Malaya.

— contains 6 poems* by the poet translated by the poet from Malay.

————. (ed.). (1988). *An anthology of contemporary Malaysian Literature*. Kuala Lumpur: Dewan Bahasa & Pustaka.

– contains 6 poems** by poet, translated by himself from the original Malay.

Maniam, K. S. & Shanmughalingam, M. (Compilers). (1988). *An anthology of Malaysian poetry*. Kuala Lumpur: Dewan Bahasa & Pustaka.

— contains 6 poems by the poet written originally in English, 5 of which are from *Time and its people*.

Soleha Ishak *et al*. (Trans). (1998). *Malaysian literary laureates: Selected works*. Kuala Lumpur: Dewan Bahasa & Pustaka.

— contains 20 poems*** translated by the poet from original Malay.

Dewan Bahasa & Pustaka. (2000). *Anthology puisi. penyair, alam dan kemanusiaan: Pengucapan puisi dunia Kuala Lumpur 2000*. Kuala Lumpur: Dewan Bahasa & Pustaka.
— contains 6 poems translated by the poet. Most of the poems have been included in the current anthology *Rowing Down Two Rivers* (2000). All 20 poems are republished in the current anthology *Rowing Down Two Rivers* (2000)

(1991). Our people must sail the seas of the world. Acceptance Speech for the National Literary Laureate Award. In Soleha Ishak *et. al.* (Trans.) Malaysian Literary Laureates. Selected works.

Muhammad Haji Salleh (July 20–22, 2001,). *Decolonisation: A personal journey*. Paper presented at a workshop organised by Dewan Bahasa & Pustaka entitled entitled "Critical views on works by Muhammad Haji Salleh".

Secondary Texts

Fadillah Merican (2003). An Interview with Muhammad Haji Salleh. In Zawiah Yahya (ed.), *Critical views on works by Muhammad Haji Salleh* (pp.12–32). Kuala Lumpur: Dewan Bahasa & Pustaka.

Checketts, S. (2003). Changed by time and place: Muhammad Haji Salleh, Yeats and the subversion of myth, symbol and legend. In Zawiah Yahya (ed.), *Critical views on works by Muhammad Haji Salleh* (pp. 244–277). Kuala Lumpur: Dewan Bahasa & Pustaka.

Raihanah Mohd Mydin & D'Cruz, V. (2000). Notions of self and home in Muhammad Haji Salleh's *Time and its people*. In S. H. Chan, M. A. Quayum & R. Talif (eds.), Diverse *voices: Readings in languages, literatures and cultures* (pp. 192-199). Serdang: Universiti Putra Malaysia.

Raihanah Mohd Mydin & D'Cruz, V. (2003). The cosmopolitanism for an early Muhammad Haji Salleh and the quest for a foundational imaginary of home. In Zawiah Yahya (ed.), *Critical views on works by Muhammad Haji Salleh* (pp. 35-53). Kuala Lumpur: Dewan Bahasa & Pustaka.

Ruzy S. Hashim. (2003). Yang empunya cerita: Muhammad Haji Salleh's revision of sejarah melayu. In Zawiyah Yahya(ed.), *Critical views on works by Muhammad Haji Salleh* (pp. 86–105). Kuala Lumpur: Dewan Bahasa & Pustaka.

Shirley Lim Geok-lin

9.0 Epigraph

The dominant imprint I have carried with me since birth was of a Malaysian homeland. It has been an imperative for me to make a sense of these birthmarks…it has taken me a longer time to leave home than most immigrants.

To give up the struggle for a memorialised homeland may be the most forgiving act I can do…

In California, I am beginning to write stories about America, as well as about Malaysia. Listening and telling my own stories, I am moving home.

—Shirley Lim Geok-lin,
Among the White Moon Faces
(1996, 347–348)

9.1 Introduction

Shirley Lim was born in December 1944 in Malacca, Malaysia into a middle-class family of an English-educated father in colonial Malaya. Lim was exposed to the English language and literature from an early age through the rigorous Catholic Convent schooling, and the English literature programme at the University of Malaya. She graduated with first class honours in 1967.

In 1969, disillusioned with the "racialised dimensions" of Malaysian political, economic, social and literary life and in pursuit of academic opportunities, Lim left Malaysia for the USA on a Fulbright scholarship. She earned her M.A. in 1971, and obtained her Ph.D. in 1973 from Brandeis University.

Lim is now an American citizen. Academic work, creative writing, marriage and motherhood, feminism and the community of the Chinese diaspora in America have all contributed to Lim's professional and personal development.

Amongst other positions, she was Chair Professor of English at the University of Hong Kong from 1999–2000. At present, she is Professor of English and Women's Studies at the University of California, Santa Barbara. She is a critically acclaimed writer and respected academician, and has been the recipient of many fellowships, residencies, prizes, awards and grants.

Her specialisation areas are 20th century American literature, minority discourses, Asian American cultural studies, postcolonial and Southeast Asian literature, feminist writing and theory, and creative writing. These fields of study reflect the intertwined personal and national circumstances and influences of an emotionally deprived childhood. Her life as a colonised subject, a Malaysian Chinese in post-independence Malaysia; a self-exiled Malaysian Chinese; a woman of colour in white mainstream America; as a writer determined to situate herself in the American national canon and US feminist discussion, and last but not least, as scholar and lover of the English language and literary studies.

Lim's critical essays, autobiographical writings, poems, and fiction on Malaysia provide insight from a particular perspective, into events, circumstances and peoples specific to the time and place in which she situates her stories—from colonial Malaya to Malaysia of the 21st century.

The characters, mainly young and old Chinese women that people her creative works, reflect the difficult everyday realities of these times. Strong and yet vulnerable, they also epitomise individuals in situations of change with the onset of Western values and modernity, caught in personal, familial and community conflicts. This large body of works is then an important component of Malaysian literary studies for it provides insight into one writer's means of self-definition, a collective product of the multiplicity of selves of a Malaysian-born transnational writer. This multiplicity of selves is seen in the characters of her writing set in Malaysia before she left for America in 1969. Although fictional creations, they are based on the personal experiences of the writer herself. Her post-1969 critical essays on Asian and Southeast Asian literature in English and her position as a writer, emphasise this point again and again.

Lim's relationship with English has been the one constant in a life of cultural diversity and conflicting values. The events of her life are interrelated and intertwined to shape the person and the perceptions, insights, opinions, subjects she writes of in her poems, her short stories, memoir, novel and critical writings: A child growing up and educated in colonial Malaya, a daughter in a large family (extended and immediate) of patriarchal priorities, a daughter growing abandoned by her mother, a postcolonial young Malaysian Chinese caught in the politics of nation-building, a postgraduate scholar in America, an "exilic/immigrant Third World woman" in America, as wife and mother and as a professional reaching out to the promise of community Anglo-American feminists offered and as Chinese/Asian writer and scholar—these are the periods of Lim's life and within each are diverse yet interlinked circumstances and effects that have shaped the writer and her work. Lim claimed English as her own language because it gave her a voice, an overpowering source of self-definition. "Unsettled and unbelonging", resisting familial, community and national priorities and caught in the "triple bind of force-fed colonial literature, cultural imperialism and denigration of ability", Lim wrote her early poems and fiction as much for self-identity as to make good her contribution to "the necessity for a literature of ones own" (See preface, Lim 1994, p. xi-xii)

A better appreciation of her creative writing is provided for in her essays and critical writings [a number brought together in one book in *Writing Southeast Asia in English: Against the Grain* (1994). The autobiographical tone provides insight into the feelings and emotions behind these works. Lim has said that, "singleness of self is an impossible project for an immigrant like me" (Gabriel, 1995,

p. 33). It is the many voices and influences of this multiplicity of selves that compels Shirley Lim to speak through the gender, racial, ethnic, cultural, personal and national elements in her works. Equally significant, the works provide ample proof of her evocative, stylish command of a language not her own.

9.2   Discussion of works

A list of Lim's publications at the time of writing, is given in the bibliography at the end of this chapter. In the last ten years or so, particularly after the publication of her memoir in 1996, and international and American attention has been strengthened, Lim has written critical books, chapters and papers, edited and co-edited volumes on new literatures in English, literature of Asian/Southeast Asian American writers, of Asian/Chinese American Women, transnational Asian writers, and discussions on the literature and culture of contemporary America. These attest to the widening of the contexts from which she writes. In the same way, her "stories about America" will increase in number but her emotional and physical contact with Malaysia, the "joss of memory" will no doubt make Lim continue to write "stories about Malaysia" in California. It would be natural to consider Lim's "earlier" writing as Malaysia-centred and Malaysia-derived, and therefore, of direct relevance to Malaysian literature in English. But it must be remembered that so much of her "American stories" and poems (of Lim in America, even of Americans) have their roots in a Malaysian past. The study of Malaysian writing in English cannot afford to ignore political-cultural issues at the local and global levels. Lim herself considers political and cultural motivations in her study on nationalism and literature in English from the Philippines and Singapore (Lim, 1993a).

The epigraph for this chapter provides a neat summary of the rationale to consider not just Lim's Malaysian works but also her made-in-America Malaysian writing. With regards to her poems, no particular anthology will be concentrated on since the four anthologies—*Crossing the Peninsular and Other Poems* [CP] (1980), *No Man's Grove and Other Poems* [NMG] (1985), *Modern Secrets: New and Selected Poems* [MS] (1989), *Monsoon History: Selected Poems* [MH] (1994)—"overlap" and provide a kind of continuity with some poems in earlier anthologies appearing in later ones. Some attention will be focused on her fiction—the short stories and especially *Joss and Gold* (2001); also to her *Memoirs of a Nyonya Feminist* [henceforth referred as *Memoirs*] and essays especially those in *Writing Southeast Asia in English: Against the Grain* (1994). The last two texts provide links to her creative writing; equally importantly they provide the socio-political context crucial to an understanding of the political and emotional stand of so many non-Malay / non-Malaysian writers and scholars of Malaysian literature in English. As such, they will be looked at first, as providing the groundwork for the poetry and fiction.

Memoirs foregrounds experiences of exclusion, marginality and dislocation as a result of being born into and seeking to break out of "the pomegranate shell of being Chinese and [a] girl". There is, however, also exclusion outside the familial level, from the tensions of Malaysian political, economic, social, sexual, racial and cultural life (Parts I and II, and Chapter 1 of Part III). *Memoirs'* American sections (Parts III and IV) also detail similar tensions of alienation.

The Malaysia-based sections (childhood, adolescence, university life and after May 13 racial riots) are held together by a narrative that reiterates alienation from conflicts arising out of male oppression, values and a socio-political context that raised questions over the construct of national identity and post-independence nation building which Lim resisted—what she saw as the "Malay bias" in every aspect of Malaysian nationalism particularly after May 1969.

Two perceptions on the title/s of the memoir need to be mentioned. *Among the White Moon Faces* is subtitled *An Asian-American Memoir of Homelands* for the publication by the New

York-based Feminist Press for its Cross-Cultural Memoir series. The release by Times Book International for the Asian region is subtitled *Memoirs of a Nyonya Feminist*. While both sub-title versions are relevant to the study of contemporary literature, they also reach out to more specific, though not mutually exclusive readership: the one for Asian American cultural studies, feminist writing and theory; the other for postcolonial and Southeast Asian literature and for the study of Malaysian literature in English. The main title *Among the White Moon Faces* is best appreciated as a reference to the way Lim's life and identity have been shaped by influence and contact in the presence of whiteness. The tendency to read "whiteness" as associated with the Anglo world, her Anglophone home life, literature and discourses is valid (Morgan, 2000). However, judging by the emphasis given to her life in Malaysia and the local version of one of the sub-titles, it would be natural to assume that the whiteness must surely also refer to the familial and local community. Indeed, "moon faces" suggest Asian face shapes!

The haunting ambivalence in contexts in which the narrative voice is positioned (America or Malacca, present or past) in her poem *Night Visions* (and from which the line "Among the white moon faces" is taken) seems to support this view. Thus, the presence of whiteness would encompass experiences of the British colonial and postcolonial presence—education, exposure to, and abiding love for English literature and the intellectual density of the Western literary heritage; and of the American experience—the community of women, and of American feminists and feminism. But "white moon faces" also suggests the pervasive presence of the Chinese community particularly of Lim's father's family. Lim, product of a Westernised father and Western education, an absent (Peranakan) mother, a robust childhood with only brothers for playmates became different, atypical, resisting, "un-Chinese", Peranakan. That the White Moon Faces "beam and grasp" suggests their influence is not always negative. Thus, the "open-endedness" to the main title of Lim's memoir allows for the difference in expected readership and reader positioning as contained in the two subtitles.

By its very intertextuality (her own poems, allusions to English literature) and the deeply-felt, frank narrative, Lim's memoir is a significant text for Malaysian literature, and for our understanding of the multicultural makeup of the Malaysian writer in English for whom "resistance"—going against the grain—has always been a feature of her life and work. Her championing of the English language, the developing of an Asian-American emphasis in her work, have not dampened in any way her identification with Malaysian/Asian life particularly with the imperative, in this globalised world, to write our own stories.

Lim's *Memoirs* portrays the self—as multiple, not unified; her works advocate the importance of interdependence and commonality as being crucial to identity and survival. These are shown in various incidents and relationships in Malaysia and America. In a series of essays written earlier and in her works, the possibilities of connection and commonality are always acknowledged despite the realities of discord. These are equally crucial considerations for the study of Malaysian literature in English.

An earlier publication (*Writing Southeast Asia in English: Against the Grain*), contains in Part One, essays that position the subject: Lim in the Malaya/Malaysian context as a daughter, a Chinese with Peranakan mother, a colonised subject, a user of the coloniser's language, as post-Independence, post-May 1969 Chinese Malaysian, an Asian immigrant and a feminist in the West. Another three essays in Part Three are critical discussions of the literary texts within the context of Malaysian culture and history. These essays are directly related to the study of Malaysian literature in English. The first four essays take a strong political stand against the political, racial, linguistic and literary marginalisations of minority communities in emergent, nation-building Malaysia. The words "against the grain" indicate the position as much of the Asian writers in their use of

English and in the subjects they choose to write on, as it is of the writer Lim herself in highlighting her peripheralised position within Malaysia's nationalistic definitions and ideology. She shows how "the identities of 'woman,' 'nation' and 'race' become constituted in texts and how texts, in turn, become re-constituted in the context of nationalism" (Lim, 1994, p. xii).

These opinions find expression in her creative writings. Lim's poetry, as do her short stories and novel, construct the experiences of Chinese Malaysians and of the Peranakan community. It is important to note that although Lim must have written some poems in Malaysia before her departure for America in 1969, the majority would have been written overseas. Thus, Lim's "Malaysian" corpus provides interesting insights into a particular niche of Malaysian writing in English—that of the Malaysian-born transnational migrant. The term "transnational" underlines the mobility, instability, and porous national borders that characterise the movements of global populations (Lim, 1992, p. 103).

Lim's poetry is an exploration of "deeply personal issues"; for example, the condition of being a woman, "the working out, inviting imagination" of familial, professional, sexual, motherhood, community and national identities. She herself acknowledges that her poems are "subjective, interior and personalised" although as a critic she believes "writing should be communal, social and political" (Nor Faridah, 2001, p. 305). Lim's poetry does not address colonial and postcolonial history directly, but because identity is formed from events private and public, the overall impression that many of Lim's personal explorations offer is that they are rooted in cultural and political specifics or larger public realities. A poem like *Bukit China* for example (*MH*, p. 3) records not just personal loss of a father, but also the loss of a country, of Chinese tradition and the dislocation from loss of community. In the same way, the trials of the *Dulang Washer* (*MH*, p. 9) are erected against a backdrop of immigrant misery and exploitation. In *Lament* (*MH*, p. 56), the choice of English is made and despite the mock-ironic bantering, the choice is made "before history and all / It makes, belonging / Rest in the soil."

Lim herself has written on the need for the Asian woman writer to claim her subjectivity by foregrounding the material self and insisting on political realism:

> For me, recognising a material self is to begin to write politically, with a sense of history and large forces at work outside the subject.
>
> (1994, p. 25)

This credo for foregrounding the material self and "leaving behind the sensual world" is seen in many of her "women poems" although Lim says her own writings:

> [H]ave hardly begun to glimpse this material self …[and] the subject expressed in them while sovereign, is diminutive and sometimes phantasmal.
>
> (1994, p. 24)

The ordered structure of *Pantoun for Chinese Women* (*MH*, p. 6) strengthens the harsh material reality faced by Chinese mothers and baby girls; in *Epitaph* (*MH*, p. 14) the divided, split woman reflects tersely on her identity, one marked by ambivalence between a strong sense of awareness and a strange absence: "She has herself and she has dust." Part of the practice of foregrounding the material self is to highlight the stranglehold of traditional social expectations on the Asian woman and her resulting circumstances. *At Forty* (*MS*, p. 40), *Divorce* (*MH*, p. 143) and *Woman's Dreams* (*MH*, p. 165) are good examples. There are, however, poems in which there are possibilities of addressing marginalisation through reaching out, being aware, taking a stand and rejecting given conditions: *I Look for Women* (*MH*, p. 166), *Queens* (*MH*, p. 127), *I Would Like* (*MH*, p. 38), *Women's Dreams* (*MH*, p. 165), *Fear and Friendship* (*MS*, p. 126).

Despite the political realism (situated in the Malaysian or American landscape), distancing and detachment through rigid structuring of the poem or clear statements, many of Lim's poems are imbued with a profound sense of loss and loneliness. This is not unlike how she describes her own life, as a simultaneous existence of proud independence and of loneliness suggesting the uneasy tension between self and community, self and country, home and the wider world. In *My Father's Sadness* (*MH*, p. 24), Lim implies distancing and absence of subjectivity:

> How hard it is to be a father,
>
> a bull under the axle,
>
> the mangrove netted by lianas, the host,
>
> perishing of its lavishness.

Yet what precedes are strongly-felt details of the familial and community ties in which he was enmeshed.

In *No Man's Grove* (*MH*, p. 37) the poet declares her difference "I choose to walk between water and land," in a 'grove' of her own. Yet poems such as the *Windscreen's Speckled View* (*MH*, p.47), *American Driving* (*MH*, p.66), *Identity No Longer* (*MH*, p.52), *Monsoon History* (*MH*, p. 52), *Visiting Malacca* (*MH*, p.32), *Returning to the Missionary School* (*MH*, p.33) are fraught with the weight and reality of history and sometimes rendering the self small, fractured and "phantasmal".

History, family, ethnic community, women and feminism—in Lim's poetry these subjects colour. But she also sheds light on the conditions of women all over the world, past and present. The various intertwined threads come together best in poems that chart moments and phases of her life whether she is talking of her father, a mother lost to her, as American immigrant with multiple identities, as a Malaysian Chinese and as a woman. These include "*My Father's Sadness*," "*Inventing Mothers*," "*Birth, Sex, Death*," "*American Driving*" and "*Bukit China*."

This brief account of Lim's poetry would be incomplete without some reference to its technical range and broad spread of subjects, the intertextuality, all of which are indicative of the rich and diverse influences on "the bookish life" of a scholar exposed very early to literature and then to literary theory and feminist studies. To the rich world of Western literary and cultural heritage is added that drawn from the plurality of the Malaysian and Asian hinterland (Lim, 1992, p. 25–26).

There are various stanzaic variations in her poetry, with the poems being mostly in free verse. There are also sonnets, poems in rhymed forms [for example *Family Album* (*MH*, p. 162)], local in form in *Malay Pantoun*, and *Pantoun for Chinese Women* and, in the use of local words in *Pidgin, Song of Old Malaya* and *Arak*. The titles of her poems indicate a rich literary store of mainstream English literature and culture: *In Memoriam, An Immigrant Looks at Whitman, Walden, On Reading Coleridge's Poem, Thoughts on a Cézanne Still Life,* and *The Painter Munch*. These poems "rub shoulders" with those in which images are drawn from the natural and political landscape of the country of her birth: *Crossing the Peninsular, No Man's Grove, Bukit China, Monsoon History* and *Render to the Young*.

Lim's second collection of short stories *Life's Mysteries: The Best of Shirley Lim* (1995) consists of all the stories previously published in the first collection, *Another Country* (1982) with the addition of four other stories *Nature's Daughter, Thirst, The Bridge* (written in 1985) and *Hunger* (1990). The earliest of the stories *Journey* was written when she was an undergraduate (1967). Other than *The Touring Company* (1968) all the other stories were written in America although a few were published in Malaysian journals. The two earliest short stories were included in *Twenty-two Malaysian Stories* (1967) and *Malaysian Short Stories* (1980) respectively, both in the Heinemann (Asia). The only short story mentioned in this chapter not in *Life's Mysteries* is *On Christmas Day in The Morning*, which is in *Malaysian Short Stories*. In 1997, *Two Dreams* was published by the Feminist Press in New York for American readers to have access to Lim's stories in book form. It contains the stories previously published between 1969–1996; the only new addition is *Sisters*, and this will be referred to later.

"These stories have autobiographical perceptions but they [are] not autobiographical fiction" (Nor Faridah, 1995 p. 78). Except for *Thirst*, all the stories revolve around a Chinese protagonist of a variety of economic and social positions reflective of the many-layered, multicultural diversity of Lim's own past and present. The *Peranakan* background features in only three of the stories, *The Haunting*, *Native Daughter* and *The Bridge*. Two stories (set in America) have protagonists, Su Yu in *A Pot of Rice* and the narrator in *Transportation in Westchester* who, although not specifically Malaysians, acquaint us with Asian experiences abroad. The protagonists, and their friends and relatives in all these stories are a motley group and are portrayed with convincing depth. Despite the diversity of specific settings, "familiar" protagonists at odds with the family and community provide a sense of continuity; for the Malaysian reader there are perspectives on the Malaysian/Malaysian Chinese landscape that are at once expected and unexpected.

There is the precocious, savvy, sensitive child, perceptive beyond her years watching adult prejudices, cruelty and isolation (*Hunger, Life's Mysteries* , *Native Daughter, The Bridge, Journey* and *On Christmas Day in the Morning*); there is the older narrator looking at herself looking at others (*The Good Old Days*); the new migrant caught between the memories and demands of two worlds (*Two Dreams, Transportation in Westchester, A Pot of Rice*). In *The Touring Company*, a student reflects on the joy and sadness she felt when she took part in a touring company's staging of *A Midsummer Night's Dream*. She is at the crossroads of choosing between security—commitment, perhaps marriage, and the excitement of a larger world. The story subtly highlights the social constraints faced by women, not only in emergent Asian countries but women everywhere. There is also the young Malaysian Chinese woman, single, financially secured, independent and lonely, yet learning to cope. The character Su Wang appears in *Haunting* and *Another*

Country and as "Wang" in *Keng Hua*. The first two stories are perhaps the only two in the collection that are happy and come close to celebrating woman's good sense and initiative of bonding between women at the emotional and intercultural levels.

Whatever the variation in narrative perspective, there is a thematic coherence in the way the women-centred texts (even in *Thirst,* the only story with a male protagonist) foreground the different conditions of being a woman. Most of these are situations of subordination, marginalisation, and victimisation ranging from the doubly-victimised *Farmer's Wife* to the various young women in *Conversations of Young Women* and *Mr. Tang's Girls* for whom oppressions result from "multiple conserving circles of authority" often maintained by women themselves.

The overall tone of these stories is one of ironic exposure of victimisation, defeatist suffering and compromised happiness. There is not the wider representation of women's condition, the use of "aware" narrative voices and ironic humour to alleviate the emptiness and fear.

Other than gender concerns, the stories are held together by the Malayan/Malaysian landscape—the sights, sounds and smells of Lim's place of birth and growing up. Local realities and atmosphere are delivered in focused, precise economy of words and images. The streets and houses of Malacca, the closed and enclosing *Peranakan* dwellings, the houses and surroundings of the Chinese protagonists from different economic levels. These are remembered and recreated by the transplanted writer.

The 1997 contexts of Lim's short stories in *Two Dreams* takes "the forms of postcolonial places: tropical Malaysia and Singapore...the lonely American cities that conceal and shelter the Asian immigrant, the spaces in between airports" (Lim's preface to *Two Dreams*, 1997; p. vi). The stories are arranged in three groups according to their central concerns: 'Girl'-stories of girlhood (eg. *Hunger, Life's Mysteries*); 'Country'—which concerns stories of interactions between different cultures and peoples (e.g. *The Bridge, The Good Old Days*); 'Woman'—which comprise stories of complex relationships between different genders, race and ethnicities (eg. *Haunting, Transportation in Westchester, Another Country*). *Sisters*, not in any of her earlier anthologies, is an excerpt from Lim's novel-in-progress as mentioned in the introduction of the anthology by Zhou Xiaojing (Lim, 1997, p. xii). There are echoes of *Mr.Tang's Girls* in the family set-up and relationships. Dark humour and plot differences point to Lim's concern to show in her novel "the paradoxes faced by young Asian and Asian American women, raised in traditional families but exposed to modern values, as they seek to take charge of their own sexualities" (Lim, 1997, p. xii).

On writing her *Memoirs* and the process of writing, selecting and editing the past as she saw it, Lim said:

I focused on the writing, on being clear rather than on self-pity, resentment or bitterness. I got into the experience of myself as a young child.

(Tan, 1996, p. 6)

In *Joss and Gold*, [henceforth referred as *Joss*], her first novel, and working in a genre that allows for freer play of creativity, we see a similar bid for fair representation of identity, gender relations, friendship against a backdrop of political upheaval and social change affecting diverse cultures over three decades. Lim does this by presenting not a single narrative perspective, but a diversity of discourses and voices. *Joss* is the only work in which Lim clearly and consistently presents issues to do with Malaysian nation-building, specifically those taken up by non-Malay Malaysians, and which Lim repeatedly mentions in her essays of the 1970s and 1980s—Malay rights, the Malay language, English, and the marginalisation of other races. The novel form allows her the space to engage in these issues and develop the drama of life in multiracial, multi-ethnic, multicultural Malaysia—its vulnerabilities and possibilities, its rich concoction of "misery" and "meanings." In an interview at the time of writing the novel, she said:

...[T]he novel is a huge strategy to incorporate a Bakhtinian dialogism. I'm able to incorporate multiple points of view, something which I have wilfully, deliberately planned... What takes place is a multiplicity of positions.

(Nor Faridah, 1995, p. 77)

Thus, a reading of the novel based on Bakhtinian terms of dialogics would do justice to it. Apart from acting on the cue given by the writer herself, other factors, gathered from her critical and autobiographical writings suggest the appropriacy of the approach.

Joss is a product of the authours "multilogical" cultural worlds indeed of so many of Asian writers writing in English. As a female, Chinese, Malayan colonised subject, postcolonial Malaysian, Peranakan, American, with systems whose values often clash, Lim very early in life understood "pluralism as the ground of experience". "Cultures (not culture), differences (not centrism)" form the basis of her enquiries and writing. Contradictions opened out counter-possibilities and raised challenging questions, divergences and "ferments" (Lim, 1992, pp. 37–38). Life in America added to the multitude of communities, questions, dialogue, voices and perspectives. But life in America also nurtured the flowering of a literary career and the extension of a readership to the Asian-American aspect of her experience. When Dennis Haskell writes of *Joss*: ...readers of any gender or culture will enjoy this book..." he acknowledges the varied and complex threads of identity and relationships of three cultures (Malaysian, American, Singapore) and its various communities, over thirteen years, encompassing a time of political and social upheavals. Indeed, the many-voiced, open-ended nature of the American novel and more specifically the multicultural perspectives of the works of transnational writers provide texts eminently suitable for Bakhtin's focus on the many voices in a text. And *Joss* is just such a text, since Bakhtin was concerned with the notion of the "addressivity" of all language. He said that, "Language is addressed to someone, never uttered without consciousness of a relationship between the speaker and the addressee"(Guerin, Labor, Morgan, Reesman & Willingham, 1999, p. 349). We need to bear in mind therefore the relationship of author to the audience/readership, of the relationship between Lim's text and the reader. Lim is politically fully American, at heart she is still Asian/Malaysian. Her novel needs to be addressed to so many groupings of readers within these two broad categories. She must thus allow for the polyphonic novel's "voice-viewpoints" rather than a monologic point of view.

What we would need to consider in *Joss* therefore, would be its polyphonic discourse, that is, the free range given to the voices of the characters with the narrator's voice being only one among many. We need to look at not merely the interaction of characters but to the significance of facts voiced to the main protagonist (Bakhtin's "hero") and to the other characters. When the various discourses are made available, then the single perspective or the authority of ideology as expressed in the single voice of the narrator is countered, that is understood in all its limitations.

At the centre of the story is Li Ann. We learn how her life is shaped by people and events and how she in turn shapes her life and empowers herself to rise above constant change and personal problems by choosing positive circumstances. As "agent" with the power of the subject, Li Ann works out her own fate or "worthwhile" life, with joss and gold, that is, with luck and material security. Li Ann's *Joss* has been one of constant change and as a colleague tells her:

> Change and security, very tricky to have both at the same time...we must always be sure that our change means more security.

(*Joss*, p. 299)

When we consider the statements, views, declarations of the many voices in the text, there is no certainty on our part (and indeed, on Li Ann's part) that her decisions and actions after the night of May 13 brought good joss just as there is no certainty of emotional happiness with Suyin acquiring two fathers.

The presentation of the novel's subjects—Malaysian identity, Malay nationalism, marital commitment and happiness, love and responsibility, agency, modernisation and development of new nations, motherhood, bonding between women—is dialogic. We have access to different, often conflicting perspectives in the exchanges between and by characters, depending on who is being addressed.

In the case of Li Ann, we know that her ability to rise above problems and make something worthwhile of her life are qualities admired by Lim herself. However, Li Ann is not the "voiceless object" of the "ideologue author's deduction". There is ambiguity in her feelings for Chester, the American father of her child. Is it love or loneliness and boredom with marriage and a diffident husband that makes her seek the American's company? Is it fear, or sexual desire that brings her to him on the night of the riots? When she is told of his plans to return to America we are told "Li Ann hated Chester then… shallow and ugly in his thinking" (*Joss*, pp. 106–107). Yet she is desolate and distraught when he leaves. In Singapore, she is curt and ironic in the briefest of exchanges with Chester. At the same time "knowing he was somewhere on the island, her body had drifted away from her, tugged by phantom sensations and yearnings" (*Joss*, p. 247).

To Ellen, her friend and almost-confidante, she is practical and logical accepting Chester's right as a father, of Suyin's right to decide. To Paroo, she is the successful, rich corporate woman; to Chester, she is "a cool and distant figure". The narrative voice tells us that she had learnt to harden herself, able "to embrace the empty depth in the glittering surface of things". Yet in her relationship with her daughter, with grandma Teh, and with Henry in Singapore, we see other aspects opposite to the proud independence:

unqualified tenderness, patience and communication: "sorrowful loneliness", "passive melancholy", and "proud independence"—which one accurately describes Li Ann? Will Li Ann be her own victim in being able to love either too little or too much? The uncertainty of what will happen to Suyin also provides yet another perspective on Li Ann.

The dialogic, open-debate aspect is brought to bear on facets of Malaysian as well as American life. Chester's "irresponsibility," his wife Meryl's hard-headed practicality and driving ambition are countered by voices that provide more magnanimous understanding of their decisions and actions as Americans and other.

Perhaps one of the more interesting aspects of the novel for Malaysians is the dialogic representation of Malaysian politics. Lim's portrayal of the sensitive issues concerned with May 13, 1969 is also polyphonically rendered. She does not renounce her own consciousness of the pre- and post-riot conditions: namely her view of the marginalisation of the Malaysian Chinese community in the name of nation building; the need to rise above racial difference. This is channelled through Li Ann (*Joss*, pp. 44–45; 52; 90; 198) and Henry (p. 44; 85). Baktin's theory suggests Lim accommodates "the consciousness of others and re-creates them in their authentic unfinalisability" (cited in Guerin *et al.*, 1999, pp. 353–354).

Statements on nationalism, loyalty, Malay rights, Chinese in Malaysia, the national language and the position of English are uttered by Abdullah (a journalist) and Samad (a radio announcer), both Li Ann's university mates. Care is taken to highlight Abdullah's genial nature and disarming frankness beside Samad's less communicative ways. We are given strongly-worded pronouncements on racial differences by Abdullah, yet in Li Ann's eyes he is "gentle, understanding, kind Abdullah". It is Abdullah who brings her home after the night with Chester; the narrative acknowledges Abdullah's "straight talking" when he chastises Chester's irresponsibility for not seeking his child sooner. We are also shown Abdullah adjusting his views on the English language (*Joss*, pp. 288–289). In portraying the sad circumstances of Paroo and Gina's relationship, the narrative mutes the strident (Abdullah), aloof (Samad) face of Malay nationalism by showing the extent of racial prejudice and conflict between other races in the country. Similarly, the enduring relationship between the friends, something that goes beyond mere contact, provides a kinder aspect of Malaysian multicultural relations.

Interestingly, Abdullah's pronouncements to Li Ann on Malaysian politics are made with no response on her part (*Joss*, p. 58) or they "peter out" in open-endedness (*Joss*, pp. 56; 69–70; 104). Indeed, the older Li Ann, at the end, comments on Bumi politics in a detached manner (*Joss*, p.237) as if "big city tolerance and anonymity" of Singapore have distanced her from issues once close to her heart. If dialogues suggest open lines and communication, then Abdullah's ambiguous, one-way monologues, and Samad's reticence and the unlimited dialogic exchanges in the earlier part of the story (e.g. *Joss*, p. 70) suggest the sensitive, closed nature of the subject, an example of "inconclusive present day reality".

Bakhtin believes that the plurality of voices of a modern novel and the avoidance of a single perspective helped counter what he called "the dangers of knowledge" inside or outside a text (cited in Guerin *et al.*, 1999, p.351). Given the autobiographical material available on Lim, Malaysian and American readers can read too much into *Joss* and equate it to her life. *Joss* is fiction, and by providing multiple voices and perspectives, Lim shows that the national identity of a transnational writer cannot be anchored to a single country. Importantly, it is Lim's effort at reciprocity to play fair to the many the worlds that have made her what she is.

9.3 Conclusion

When we talk about Shirley Lim's works, we are dealing with writing that is both Malaysian and international in focus, relevance, readership and accessibility. Few Malaysian writers can lay claim to so many "identities", or to the conflict of interests that can arise from this. It is this rich diversity of voices from Lim's creative and academic writing that has enriched the literature of our corner of the world. Although she is moving into the Chinese-American literary and feminist niche, it seems logical to expect her to continue to write and tell her "own stories" from those aspects of her self that are predominantly (but always never wholly) Malaysian.

Bibliography

Primary Sources

Lim, S. G. (1980). *Crossing the peninsular and other poems*. Kuala Lumpur: Heinemann Asia.

————. (1982). *Another country and other stories*. Singapore: Times Books International.

————. (1985). *No man's groove and other poems*. Singapore: National University of Singapore English Department Press.

————. (1985). The dispossessing eye: Reading Wordsworth on the equatorial line. In P. Hyland (ed.), *Discharging the canon: Cross cultural readings in literature* (n.p). Singapore: Singapore University Press.

————. (1988). Voices from the hinterland: Plurality and identity in the national literatures from Malaysia and Singapore. *World literature written in English 28*(1), (pp.145–153).

————. (1989). *Modern secrets: New and selected Poems*. Aarhus & London: Dangaroo Press.

————. (1991). Malaysia and Singapore. In B. King (ed.), *The Commonwealth novel since 1960* (pp. 87–104). New York:Macmillan.

————. (1992). *Writing Southeast Asia in English: Against the grain*. London: Skoob Books Publishing Ltd.

————. (1992). *Reading the literature of Asian America*. Philadelphia; Temple University Press.

————. (1993). Gods who fail: Ancestral religions in the new literatures in English from Malaysia and Singapore. In C. Y. Loh and I. K. Ong (eds.), *Southeast Asia writes back!Skoob Pacifica anthology No. 1* (pp. 224–237). London: Skoob Books Publishing Ltd.

Lim, S. G. & Spencer, N. A. (eds.). (1993). *One world of literature*. Boston: Houghton Mifflin.

Lim, S. G. (1994). *Monsoon history: Selected poems*. London: Skoob Books Publishing Ltd.

———. (1995). *Life's mysteries: The best of Shirley Lim*. Singapore: Times Books International.

———. (1996). *Among the white moon faces: Memoirs of a nyonya feminist*. Singapore: Times Books International. (Published as *Among the white moon faces: An Asian American memoir of homelands*. New York: Feminist Press.)

———. (1997). *Two dreams: Short stories*. New York: Feminist Press.

———. (2001). *Joss and gold*. Singapore: Times Books International.

Secondary Sources

Alina Rastam. (1996, September 4). A life worth reading. *New Straits Times*, (p. 6).

Gabriel, S.P. (1995, March 1). The many selves of an Asian writer. *New Straits Times*, (p. 33).

Guerin, W. L., Labor, E., Morgan, L., Reesman, J.C., & Willingham, J.R. (1999). *A handbook of critical approaches to literature* (4th ed). New York: Oxford University Press.

Koh, T. A. (2001). On the margin, in whose canon? The situation of Ee Tiang Hong and Shirley Lim. In M. A. Quayum & P. Wicks (eds.), *Malaysian literature in English: A critical reader* (pp.111–123). Petaling Jaya: Longman.

Morgan, N. (2000). Shirley Geok-Lin Lim. In G. Huang (ed.), *Asian American autobiographies: A bio-bibliographical critical sourcebook* (pp.276–284). Westport, Connecticut: Greenwood Press.

Nor Faridah Abdul Manaf (1995). "More than just a woman" [Interview with Shirley Lim Geok-lin]. *Tenggara, 34*, (pp. 75–86).

Nor Faridah Abdul Manaf & Quayum, M. A. (2001). *Colonial to global: Malaysian women's writing in English: 1940s–1990s*. Kuala Lumpur: International Islamic University Malaysia.

Wong, P. N. (1992, April 1). The consequence of their choice, *New Straits Times*, (p. 35).

————. (1998). Reading two women's narratives: Sold for silver and Among the white moon faces. In Luisa J. Mallari-Hall, L. Rose & X. Tope (eds.), *Texts & Contexts* (pp. 148–65). Quezon City, Philipines: University of the Philippines, Department of English and Comparative Literature.

K.S. Maniam

10.0 Epigraph
The emergence of this story ["Ratnamuni"] reveals, as I
mentioned earlier, the conversion of a literary event into
a commonly felt truth about the individual and society.
To achieve this I have had recourse to three kinds of
phenomena: personal history, communal and national
history and, finally, an awareness in the individual that
transcends both, which I call a mystical experience of
the larger personality that resides within us.

— K. S. Maniam
(Cited in Quayum & Wicks, 2001, p. 265)

10.1 Introduction
K. S. Maniam was born in Bedong, Kedah in 1942. He is a Tamil
Hindu, a descendent of a former migrant who came to Malaya from
India around 1916. His father was a laundryman for the local
hospital and the parents also tapped rubber at a nearby estate. The
familiar scene of living in a hospital compound and observing the
estate worker's lifestyle became the introduction to his sense of
understanding of the Indian community which would form the
basis of his first novel *The Return.*

He began his primary education in a Tamil school but after a
year, continued in English at the Ibrahim School in Sungai Petani,
Kedah. After the completion of his schooling, Maniam became a
student-teacher for a few months before leaving for India to study
medicine. However, a year later, he left India for Britain, changing
his area of studies to Education. He received his Certificate of
Education from the Malayan Teachers College in Wolverhampton,
Britain in 1964, and later, taught for several years in secondary
schools in Kedah. He then continued his studies at the University

of Malaya where he received his Bachelors degree in 1973, and later his Masters degree in 1979 with a thesis entitled "A Critical History of Malaysian and Singaporean Poetry in English". Upon completing his graduate studies, he became a faculty member of the English Department, as a lecturer between 1980 and 1986, and as an Associate Professor between 1987 and 1997. He has since retired from academia and is now a full-time writer.

K. S. Maniam is a versatile writer who manages to transcendent the major genres of literature to produce poems, plays, short stories, novels and essays. He began writing poetry in the 1960s and early 1970s. His poems were first published in the *Singapore Straits Times*. In the latter part of 1970s, he began experimenting with prose. His short stories—*Ratnamuni, The Third Child, The Dream of Vasantha* and *Removal in Pasir Panjang* — appeared in the anthology of *Malaysian Short Stories* in 1981. In the same year, he published his first novel, *The Return*, the story of Ravi and his migrant family which critics have said is in fact a semi-autobiography. In 1984, his play, *The Cord*, which was published the previous year, was staged in Kuala Lumpur. *The Sandpit* was staged in Singapore in 1991, and was restaged three years later in Kuala Lumpur at a festival celebrating his theatrical works entitled "A Festival of K. S. Maniam's Plays". The following year, in 1995, *Skin Trilogy* was staged at the National Art Gallery in Kuala Lumpur. In 1993, he produced his second novel, *In a Far Country*, and in between continued to publish short stories in numerous national and international publications such as the 1988 publication *Encounters: Selected Indian and Australian Stories*, and the 1992 *Rim of Fire: Stories from the Pacific Rim*. His long awaited third novel, *Between Lives* was published in 2003.

His corpus of work has won him awards and accolades, both within the country and internationally. He won the first prize for the 1987 and 1990 *The NST*-Shell Short Story Competition for *The Loved Flaw* and *Haunting the Tiger*, respectively. In October 2000, he was awarded the Raja Rao Award for outstanding literary contribution by a South Asian diaspora, instituted by the Samvad India Foundation.

The opening quote in the prologue illustrates K. S. Maniam's twofold strength: "His awareness of the different contributive aspects to an individual's sense of history regardless of his/her socio-cultural and national background. And, more importantly, his effort at transcending these areas of human experience—the personal, communal, national and even mystical—in creating works of fiction that speak of "commonly felt truth[s]" (*ibid.*) to the individual and communities, and even nations at large, without losing his sense of purpose as a writer."

Growing up in the estates of Bedong, Maniam's sense of self is deeply rooted in his socio-cultural environment. Most of his fiction be it short stories, plays or novels, delve into the psyche of the Malaysian Indian community, more specifically the estate dwellers. He speaks directly of and to them, as they form his immediate sense of history, or as he says in the article "Fiction into fact, fact into fiction: a personal reflection", "[they are] what he knows best" (*ibid*, p. 264).

However, he also admits that he is not a mere communal centered writer whose literary interests are geared at "promoting a communal outlook" (*ibid.*, p. 264). Maniam prides himself as a writer who knows his sense of direction, in particular in his approach to his art. As the above quote illustrates, he is governed by the need to appreciate and understand the individual in his/her holistic sensibilities. As a writer, Maniam comes to grips with the universal and global issues of man and society through the representation of the "immediate and local preoccupations" of his community (*ibid*).

10.2 Discussion of works
This section presents some of K. S. Maniam's corpus of short stories, novels and plays vis-à-vis elements of fiction, and discusses the

extent to which the writer has enriched our appreciation of literary work in Malaysia.

To begin with, the setting of his works highlights Maniam's Malaysia, in particular the Bedong estates, which was an integral part of his childhood landscape. His first novel *The Return* is set primarily in the estates of Kedah. In tracing the settings of Maniam's fiction, readers will discover an apparent pattern as many of them are set in Kedah; such as *The Eagles* and *We Make it to the Capital*, which are set in Sungei Petani; *The Aborting*, set in Langkawi and Kuala Lumpur; and *Ratnamuni*, his first published short story, set in Bedong. Kedah is to Maniam, what Malgudi was to R. K. Narayan. It's the creative landscape that occupies his fictions.

In terms of narrative voice, Maniam lends his creativity to both female and male personas. In *Ratnamuni*, we are introduced to the Muniandy who questions the true father of his son. On the other hand, in *In Flight*, the protagonist is Samantha de Silva, a girl who spends her days between hanging out at airports dreaming that she is an air stewardess, and later on at bars enjoying the attention she gets from the men that come by. Both stories use the dramatic monologues, giving the reader a taste of the different personas Maniam is capable of creating. The following two quotes from *Ratnamuni* and *In Flight*, respectively, illustrate the narrative voices in Maniam's fiction:

> Repot-kept, Ayah. I cannot tell straight. This Bedong I stay all my life I did not come straight. "Ma-la-ya" I was hearing all the time. My son I have now. When I was coming here— nothing. Only her—the uduku. ...destination-mastination. This land here I can hold in the palm of my hand.

(1994, p. 1)

I love my voice. When I speak silk seems to be pouring out of my throat: rich, soft and caressing. Ma hates my speaking from the top of my chest. …my boobs certainly come from her. Hope to God they don't turn into mushy soursops when I get older!

(1996, p. 22)

The differences in the above excerpts illustrate the writer's versatility in positioning his characters from different social and cultural backgrounds. Muniandy's working class Manglish is a contrast to Sam's "pretentious" English. Maniam's representations of the different communities be it in terms of race or social status add to the realism of his narration. A critic describes Maniam's use of English in *The Cord* as infusing "words with a rhythm that was identifiably Indian" (1983, p. 134).

Maniam's writing is also filled with appropriation of the English language in order to fit the nuances of the culture and community he writes on and from (Roxas-Tope, 1998, p. 105–106). His liberal use of "untranslated" words like *kolam, kumkum, uduku, lallang, parang, thundu, ayoh, periatai, ayah* and *amah*, to name but a few, give his English fictions an unquestionable sense of belonging to Malaysia. As Roxas-Trope states, "Localised English can now be viewed as a product of a writer's desire to make writing accessible and rooted to local culture"(*ibid.*, p. 105).

An important aspect of the "local culture" can also be traced in Maniam's use of realism and naturalism. The subject matter of his writing highlights the concerns of everyday people especially the issues relevant to the migrant Tamil community in Malaysia. Maniam provides a vivid depiction of what life must have been for the early migrant community in the estates whilst the labourers struggle to find a sense of belonging in the adopted land. The depiction of the everyday issues haunting the estate dwellers range from poverty, alcoholism and illiteracy to marital problems, family conflicts and the caste system. A good example of the range of issues faced by the estate occupants can be seen in Maniam's semi-autobiography *The Return*. The novel, first published in 1981, presents readers to the plethora of conflicts faced by the protagonist, young Ravi, Malayan born and English-colonial educated. The struggle he endures at the hands of his fellow Tamils to overcome such an oppressive environment in order to find his sense of space and self is synonymous with the struggles faced by the migrant communities.

Maniam is also known to experiment with literary techniques in all three genres of fiction—short stories, plays and novels. His use of dream and flashbacks in many of his works allow for a more complex plot and undoubtedly, challenging read. Many of his protagonists journey back into their past in search of some sense of truth, and consequently, a sense of self. In *Haunting the Tiger*, the old Muthu travels in and out of his past in a dream state at his deathbed. By fleshing out the important memories of his life, Muthu attempts to project the psyche of his younger self, and consequently, to come to terms with his inadequacies and limitations. When Muthu tries to travel deep into the jungle to seize the tiger, a symbolic spirit of the land, his companion, the Malay Zulkifli expresses the kind of attitude Muthu needs to have:

> "There's something foreign to the tiger's nose. He won't show himself until the smells are gone."…"Mind and body smells." …"Not in the way you can't go near a person." … "The clothes you wear, the thoughts you think."…"They must fit into the place where the tiger lives."
>
> "Why must they fit in?" Muthu says. "I only want to break out from my father's hold on me."
>
> "So you brought a purpose with you?" Zulkifli says. "And a way of thinking. How can you get into the tiger's stripes and spirit?"

(1996, p. 45)

In his second novel, *In a Far Country*, Maniam continues the experimentation and the theme of finding a sense of belonging with the incorporation of a complex wed of binaries. As Peter Wicks sums up, "Public and private, past and present, dream and consciousness, present and flashback, light and dark, variously succeed each other in a whirl of juxtaposition" (Wicks, 1998, p. 61). In *In a Far Country*, Rajan a successful businessman tries to resolve some unsettled issues within himself as a descendant of a migrant community coming to terms with his sense of belonging to the adopted land. This particular novel showcases the author's sense of experimentation with characters as he provides clear possible cultural collisions of individuals from different ethnic heritage. There's Zulkifli, the Malay man who takes Rajan into the interior to face the tiger, and there's Lee Shin, a private yet multitalented Chinese man who faces similar challenge to find attachment to the land while hanging on to his racial heritage.

There is strong evidence of intertextuality between *Haunting the Tiger* and *In a Far Country*. The protagonist of the latter undertakes a mythical quest into the depths of his soul, and the land similar to that of the former's search for a sense of attachment. The symbolic spirit of the land, the tiger, is also brought back to life in the novel in order for Rajan to discover a new sense of self. And the Malay Zulkifli, again tries to assist the hero in his journey. The constant struggle between letting go of the self in order to be at one with the land, on one hand, and the fear of losing one's personality, on the other, is a real and never ending tension in both protagonists. Perhaps the recurrent images and thematic concern highlight the author's own search for answers. As Maniam ("In search of a centre," p. 14) admits, *In a Far Country* "raises more questions than provides answers".

Maniam's continued experimentation in literary production can also be seen in his plays. His critically-acclaimed plays such as *The Cord*, *The Cord* (Playlet), *The Sandpit: A Monologue* and *The Sandpit Womensis* highlight the playwright's ability to experiment with different theatrical techniques and literary concerns. *The Cord* is a story about a man trying to unearth his past to discover the true parentage of his son. (Again, Maniam incorporates intertextuality taking on the same plot line as his first published short story *Ratnamuni*). In *The Cord*, the playwright incorporates creative use of cultural symbols like the *uduku* and the *thundu*, and lighting and trance giving it the particularities that critics consider to be "firmly rooted... in Asia" (K.S. Maniam, 1994, p. 134).

The Sandpit: A Monologue and the reworked version, *The Sandpit: Womensis* are two minimalist productions that focus on female voice and characterisation. The former is a monodrama with one of two wives of a man speaking her mind about the husband and the other woman. In the latter, we are introduced to both wives as they stand on the same stage but in different settings, voicing their thoughts about their husband's, life. Each feels they know their husband better than the other. As Santha, one of the wives says of the other wife, "Sumathi sees only the outside of you, your body. I go inside and can become you" (*ibid.*, p. 213).

Maniam's plays have been a challenge for the director, actors and audience. Krishen Jit acknowledges that *The Sandpit: Womensis*, defies "all the standard rules of drama, and it fights against the normal expectations of the audience what they are used to in a play" (ibid., p. 217.) A review of *The Sandpit: Womensis* explains the levels of success the play has transcended:

> Maniam's script has, in certain sections, the poetry and passion of the classics; while at the same time possessing an ethereal quality that often threatens to occlude the audience from becoming too involved in the emotional aspects of the play. At times one is left wanting to linger on certain moments bit his writing, strongly interpreted by Krishen's direction, doesn't allow the audience the luxury of wallowing. Instead, on is jolted out of one emotion into another with barely any breathing space.
>
> (*ibid.*, p. 169–170)

An important aspect of Maniam's writing technique lies in his use of motif or recurrent image. Being predominately set around the lives of the Indian community, reader's will not be short of examples of cultural motifs in his fictions. From statues of gods like that of Nataraja which becomes the family heirloom in *The Return*, and the striking *uduku* that reveals to Muniandy the secrets of his past in *The Cord*, to the colours of the *kolams* which decorate Maniam's stories, these cultural artifacts are not mere objects but have symbolic representations. For example in *Ratnamuni* the *uduku*, according to Maniam in an essay, symbolises "the soul not only of an individual, Muniandy, but also of a people as well"(cited in Quayum and Wicks, 2001, p. 265).

Even the names of his characters are rooted in Hindu Mythology. There's Ganesh, named after the Lord Ganesh, in *Dream of Vasantha*, a young boy who takes his mother's love and attention for granted after the death of his father; there is also Kali and Lakshmi, two Hindu goddesses, who become character names in his play *The Cord*. In a review, Maniam's "audacious, know-all, carnal Kali" (Maniam, 1994, p. 99) was said to exhibit "worldly pragmatism [which] trivialises even her religious observances into a spurious variety of voo-doo" (*ibid.*, p. 139).

In terms of characterisation, Maniam's protagonists come from a varied socio-cultural background. However, as he tells Kee Thuan Chye in an interview, his preoccupation with the working class is real, as through their lives one gets to understand "what the human personality is about" (Kee, 1992, p. 15).

Maniam's women are given the space and time in accordance with the cultural environment of their communities. Some are shown to break the gender barrier which tries to curb their freedom, for instances Sumathi's great grandmother in *Kling Kling Woman*. Others continue to work within the cultural-religious prescriptions they live by. For example, in *Dream of Vasantha*, the protagonist Vasantha is shown to continue living up to the vow she made upon her husband's death to stay true to him and not allow any other man touch her. There are still others who become icons in their community and family, giving the next generation a role model to emulate. Such a character is Periatai, the grandmother in *The Return*. The female characters in Maniam's works showcase a sense of agency that is indicative of the culture and environment they live in. Some continue to struggle within themselves and their cultural space, failing to achieve emancipation such as Mala in *Mala*. Others are caught in domestic restrictions as wives and "resident sister-in-laws" where the two are in relationship with the same man; such plots can be read in *The Rock Melon* and *The Loved Flaw*. Regardless of the story line, each of the female characters move in and out of the cultural space set by the community finding their sense of voice and identity.

The thematic concerns of Maniam's works are as vast as his corpus. In his own words, Maniam positions his fiction within the framework of the "Indian philosophy and religious belief" and how it can be "modified to suit new lands, peoples and customs" (Quayum & Wicks, 2001, pp. 80–81). Speaking of Ravi's father, Naina, in *The Return*, the migrant is seen as bridging the gap between the land he was born in and the one he adopts and has come to accept as his own. This is the "ultimate in Malaysian immigrant's ambition" (*ibid.*). There are a number of texts that deal with this issue as presented previously, such as the two novels *The Return, In a Far Country*, and many of the short stories like *Ratnamuni, Haunting the Tiger* and the *Arriving*, and the play *The Cord*.

In addition, Maniam is also very concerned with the importance of the "self" and the many facets of the self that enrich our lives. He describes the thematic concern of his works as dwelling on "the death of the self —the falling away of a personality as it had been known—and being replaced by a paradigmatic self that is capable of encompassing more" (Kee, 1992, p. 14). Many of his stories fall into this category. His protagonist may leave home and travel to a different place to search for a sense of self as Ravi does in *The Return* or leave home to travel deep into the jungle to find a sense of belonging to the land as does Rajan in *In a Far Country,* and Muthu in *Haunting the Tiger,* or undertake to travel back into his past to better understand his family as Muniandy does in *The Cord.* Ultimately, each character finds his own way to discover his sense of self, successfully or otherwise.

10.3 Conclusion

Maniam's place in the Malaysian literary tradition is as undisputed as his rich corpus of short stories, plays, novels, essays and criticisms. His critical thoughts along with his fiction give him the voice he needs to address Malaysians about issues that are pertinent to the Malaysian Indian community and the nation at large. As a Malaysian writer who is also his own critic, Maniam uses his writing as a tool to discover himself, to know "what is within him" (*ibid.*). This need to discover is taken a step further when the writer sets out intentions he wishes to surpass in discovering the true value of the self. As he tells Kee Thuan Chye (*ibid.*, p. 16), "I want to see how many personalities can be contained in one self. I want to see the universe in man. I want to see the world in a broader sense. ...I know it sounds like a lofty idea but the feeling is very down-to earth. I feel it very strongly." As long as his rich creative psyche continues to search out answers for the questions his conscious mind sets out to discover, Malaysians can be assured of a significant voice they can be proud of in their community.

Bibliography

Primary Texts

Maniam, K. S. (1981). *The return*. Kuala Lumpur: Heinemann Asia.

———. (1992). A cultural potpourri. *CRNLE reviews journal, 1*, (pp.79–82).

———. (1992, June 3). Moving through cultural frontiers. *New Straits Times*, (n.p).

———. (1993). *In a far country*. London: Skoob Books Publishing Ltd.

———. (1993, December 23). Towards a Malaysian short story tradition. *New Straits Times*, (n.p).

———. (1994, September). *In search of a centre*. Paper delivered at a seminar on "Malaysian writing: The writers speak," during the 26th Singapore International Festival of Book Fair, Singapore.

———. (1994).*Sensuous horizons. The stories and the plays* London: Skoob Books Publishing Ltd. (Original work published 1983).

———. (1995). *Arriving—and other stories*. Singapore: Times Books International.

———. (1996). *Haunting the tiger*. London: Skoob Books Publishing Ltd.

———. (2000). A distracting glow [Malaysian Issue]. *Kunapipi: The journal of postcolonial writing XXII*(1), (n.p).

———. (2001). Fiction into fact, fact into fiction: a personal reflection. In M. A. Quayum & P. Wicks (eds.), *Malaysian literature in English* (pp. 263–268). Malaysia: Longman.

———. (2001). The Malaysian novelist: Detachment or spiritual transcendence?. In M. A. Quayum & P. Wicks (eds.), *Malaysian literature in English: A critical reader* (pp. 80–84). Malaysia: Longman

———. (2003). *Audrey's promise*. Petaling Jaya: Maya Press.

———. (2003). *Between lives*. Petaling Jaya: Maya Press.

———. (2003). *Escape from module H 7953*. Petaling Jaya: Maya Press.

———. (2003). *Poison pen*. Petaling Jaya: Maya Press.

———. (2003). *Steel finger*. Petaling Jaya: Maya Press.

———. (2003). *Strange journey*. Petaling Jaya: Maya Press.

———. (2003). *The dragon lives again* . Petaling Jaya: Maya Press.

————. (2003). *The lost boys*. Petaling Jaya: Maya Press.

————. (2003). *The man who understood rocks*. Petaling Jaya: Maya Press.

————. (2003). *The treasure trunk*. Petaling Jaya: Maya Press.

————. (2003). *The well*. Petaling Jaya: Maya Press.

Secondary texts

Kee, T. C. (1992). *Just in so many words: Views reviews & other things*. Singapore: Heinemann Asia.

Roxas-Tope, L. R. (1998). *(Un)framing Southeast Asia. Nationalism and postcolonial text in English in Singapore, Malaysia and the Philippines*. University of Philipines Office of Research Co-ordination.

Wicks, P. (1998, Winter). Malaysia as myth in K.S. Maniam's In a far country. *Asian culture quarterly, XXVI*(4), (n.p). In Quayum, M. A. & Wicks, P. (eds.). (2001) *Malaysian literature in English: A critical reader*. Malaysia: Longman.

Tang, S. P. (2001). Ralph Ellison and K. S. Maniam: Ethnicity in America and Malaysia, Two kinds of invisibility. In M. A. Quayum & P. Wicks (eds.), *Malaysian literature in English: A critical reader* (pp. 276–289). Malaysia: Longman.

Wicks, P. (2001). Another Malaysia: Maniam's short stories. In M. A. Quayum & P. Wicks (eds.), *Malaysian literature in English: A critical reader*. (n.p). Petaling Jaya: Longman.

Yong, M. (2001). Ring of cosmic fire: Temporal strategies and narrative consciousness in "The return." In M. A. Quayum & P. Wicks (eds.), *Malaysian literature in English: A critical reader* (n.p). Malaysia: Longman.

Kee Thuan Chye

11.0 Epigraph

Actor / M : Wait a minute. Is this how it really happened in History?

Actor / S : History? What History? We are creating fiction, Yatim. This is fiction. History is fiction.

Actor / M : What is historical truth, Mano?

Actor / S : Truth depends on who is telling the history and what he is trying to get across who his audience is. History can be manipulated to convey opposing truths. It can be distorted.

Actor / M : So how do we tell what is real truth?

—Kee Thuan Chye,
*We Could **** Mr. Birch*
(1994, p. 3)

11.1 Introduction

Kee Thuan Chye was born on May 25, 1954 in Penang. He received primary school education at Francis Light School, and his secondary education at Penang Free School. He is a graduate of the Science University of Malaysia (USM), Penang and majoring in Literature. He also holds an M. A. in Literature (Drama) from Essex University which he accomplished on a British Council Fellowship.

Kee Thuan Chye has been a journalist since 1977 when he joined the *The National Echo* in Penang as Literary Editor. In 1979, he migrated to Kuala Lumpur and joined *The New Straits Times* (*NST*), starting first as a sub-editor, then moving up to Entertainment

Editor in 1983. He wrote a weekly review column called "Cinemagoing" from 1980 to 1984, and occasionally contributed to *Asiaweek, Far Eastern Economic Review,* and *The Asia Magazine*. He also authored a weekly column on arts for *Business Times* from 1986 to 1987. He later became *NST*'s Literary Editor, having completed the full. Currently, Kee Thuan Chye is an editor with Malaysia's another English language daily, *The Star*.

Kee Thuan Chye is a journalist with a talent for drama, acting, and directing. His first love is the theater and has devoted much time to involvement in theater. As such, his writings on and for theatre are informed and founded in experience. His published writings include:

- *1984, Here and Now,* a play attacking political oppression and racial discrimination. The play is an adaptation of George's Orwell classic novel, *1984;*
- *The Big Purge* (1987) written in response to the Malaysian Government's detention of more than 100 people under the International Security Act (ISA) in October 1984;
- *We Could * * * * You, Mr. Birch* (henceforth referred as *Birch*), a satire on power, the pursuit on self-interest, the clash of Eastern and Western cultures, and the questionable role of history as a record of truth;
- The biography of a German doctor, Sir Dr. Joseph Wolf entitled *Old Doctors Never Fade Away* ;
- An anthology of short stories which he edited—*Haunting the Tiger & Other Stories.*
- *Just In So Many Words* in 1992, a collection of his views, reviews and other things.
- *A Sense of Home* in *The Merlion and the Hibiscus.*
- *A Long Way from Hollywood* in *Siverfish New Writing 2.*

As a writer of poetry, he has had his poems included in *An Anthology of Malaysian Poetry/Antologi Puisi Pelbagai Kaum* as well as in newspapers, magazines and literary journals at home and abroad.

Kee Thuan Chye's directorial ventures include K.S. Maniam's *The Birch and the Rod*; Ionesco's *Rhinoceros*; the Kabuki play, *Narukami*; Chikamatsu's *The Battles of Coxinga*, *Madame Mao's Memories*; Shakespeare's *Macbeth*;and his own plays.

As a stage actor he has played a range of roles including Creon in Anouilh's *Antigone*, Willy Loman in *Death of a Salesman*, the lead role of the mentally retarded Bill in the Australian play *Gulls*, Thomas Cromwell in *A Man for All Seasons*, and in specially created roles in Malaysian plays like K.S. Maniam's *The Cord*, Nordin Hassan's *Anak Tanjung*, Chin San Sooi's *Yap Ah Loy*. In 1987, he performed Kuo Pao-kun's one-man play *The Coffin is too Big for the Hole* to private audiences because the play was refused a public performance permit. He has also ventured into acting in the small and silver screens. His credits include speaking roles in the movies *Anna and the King* and *Entrapment* and televison drama roles in *City of the Rich*, *Kopitiam* and *Phua Chu Kang*.

Kee Thuan Chye has won significant recognition for his writing. He was a recipient of the Australian Cultural Award and served as a judge of the Commonwealth Writers Prize for the South east Asian and South Pacific Region.

Kee Thuan Chye has genuine concerns for Malaysia and taken his own steps to help create a truly Malaysian nation. He believes in racial integration and thoughts are occupied with the notion of a Malaysian identity. To this end he has named his children with Malay, Indian and Chinese names—Soraya Sunitra Kee Xiang Yin and Jebat Arjuna Kee Jia Liang. According to him, this is his contribution towards integration and the Malaysian nation. Such is Kee Thuan Chye's conviction to this cause that almost all his works conduct explorations and examinations on challenges to national integration and assert the need for a socially evolved Malaysian race.

Being educated in the theories and practice of drama, Kee Thuan Chye has produced many plays throughout his life. The knowledge and experience gained while studying at these universities have enabled him to explore the full potential of techniques and styles in drama.

Kee Thuan Chye also claims to be influenced by watching James Bond movies when he was young. When he was in Standard Six (1964) the first James Bond movie *Dr. No* was released. He was very taken by the movie and became a big fan of James Bond. He bought every novel written by Ian Flemming (James Bond) and read each one of them. Of course, he also tried to write his own novel.

A similar experience which influenced him greatly in pursuing a career in writing was watching his school production of Shakespeare's *As You Like It*. According to him, he fell in love not so much with Shakespeare but with the actress playing the lead role, Rosalind. She was probably about seventeen years old and he, eleven. This led him to read the play again and even attempt to write his own Shakespearean play. This was the turning point in his life where dramas and plays captured his heart. From this point onwards he was committed to drama as his chosen medium of literary expression.

His vast and extensive travels also contributed in motivating and influencing him to write. In 1976, he participated in a creative writing workshop at a university in the Philippines. It was his first time out of Malaysia, and the experience greatly motivated him. He experienced culture shock upon seeing how Americanised the Filipinos were. The experience raised questions within him about cultural imperialism and cultural reality, and his own situation regarding the matter. After that, he felt the need to assert his Asian self. He began to consciously search for things Asian, that could represent at least a part of him in his writing. It marked a new phase in his development.

Reading the works of other authors played a very significant role in enhancing Kee Thuan Chye's passion for writing. When he was an undergraduate, he was strongly influenced by his university reading of Samuel Beckett, Harold Pinter and Ionesco. These playwrights were instrumental in influencing him to write plays that were absurd and dealt with the world that had lost its meaning. He found instant affinity and identified easily with the portrayals of the world without meaning and people confronting despair, a world of nightmare; and a language that no longer made sense.

Kee Thuan Chye's plays almost always carry a political voice. His voice is marked by his perceptions and experiences of the late 1960s when racial politics br ought about widespread social polarisation. He witnessed during this period the ramming through of constitutional amendments, and the frequent use of the International Security Act (ISA). This made him more aware of social injustices. He was disturbed by the lack of freedom of speech and emergence of the phenomenon of self-censorship. These influenced him to write plays like *1984, Here & Now* and *The Big Purge* because he felt that every Malaysian should know the "truth" about what is going on. He took it upon himself to be the voice of the "the victims" of these circumstances, a voice that carried strong calls for social and political justice.

11.2 Discussion of works

Many of Kee Thuan Chye's major works stem from thoughts of and reactions to the "traumatic riots of May 13, 1969 which polarised race relations in Malaysia, promoted the political and educational rights of *Bumiputras* and marginalised the other races" (Robert Yeo, 1994, p. 4). This tragedy gave Kee Thuan Chye's a new perspective on life and urged him to write things which concerned human rights, racial integration, freedom, justice and equality. Along with that he brought to fore the issues of sensitivities, self-censorship, and the right to express oneself.

His play *1984, Here & Now,* is an expression of the "frustration" of an underdog class; defined not by social status or a class stratification but by racial category, even in a country where the government promotes and claims racial integration. In an interview with De Silva and Liging, Kee Thuan Chye says:

I feel that these are the things that have to be addressed particularly to the society in this time before it gets out of hand. So that is why I write politically to make people aware, to debate it, to get people to talk about it more openly. Of course it had landed me into trouble a few times but then that is the price that one has to pay.

(1995, p. 21)

Apart from this, Kee Thuan Chye also writes about things that move him—racism, unequal opportunities, backwardness, about people closing themselves up, and about curbs to freedom of speech and expression. As Thuan Chye says:

We have languished in the hope that someday, things will be different and we will finally be allowed to speak up. That day may never come without our working towards it. Which is why if anything needs to be said, it has to be said here and now. Otherwise tomorrow will be lost.

(*The Sunday Mail* ,1985, p. 30)

Hence, it is obvious that he tackled Malaysian themes such as racial discrimination and extremism, political manipulation, detention, "Big Brotherism", through use of language and with characters that were recognisably Malaysian. Kee Thuan Chye used the Malaysian context as his source of ideas and issues to be talked about, criticised and written on. Malaysia provided both the "subject-matter" for his plays, and the object of his searching—courageous political criticism. Political agenda had become his primary concern. The plays *1984, Here & Now* and *The Big Purge* (1988) are all inspired by real events that happened in Malaysia. They are about extremism, ethnic tension and their results on Malaysian society.

Kee Thuan Chye prefers the satirical mode to writings. It seems to be the way in which he can convey messages more immediately and bitingly. *The Big Purge* (1988) for example, is a savage political satire and, like many satirical writing, is didactic. Kee Thuan Chye is concerned on how important it is to conduct national policy and indeed personal relations based on tolerance despite racial differences by revealing the agenda of politicians. The early Kee Thuan Chye has always refused to self-censor himself and the result is a play which appears to be a paradox to the "total censorship" practice in Malaysia. By staging the play, Kee Thuan Chye actually reveals his most secret thoughts. He views the performance of the play as the only medium of conveying messages, and his thoughts to the Malaysian people.

His last play *Birch* concerns a historically significant event in Malaysia's imperial past. The story is carefully wound around the killing of the British Resident, J. W. W. Birch as a result of his attempt to enforce British law upon the Malay Chiefs in Perak who practised the feudal system. The play transforms illusion into reality by juxtaposing events in the past with that in the present. The actors and actresses are both themselves (as in real life), as well as the characters they play. Through the play, we see how Kee Thuan Chye binds time by presenting the past, present and future as continous stream. The play deals with power. Through this play, Kee Thuan Chye tells the audience while the identities of the power brokers may change through time and situations, the power play for the advancement of self-interest will not. And so history repeats itself.

Presently, Kee Thuan Chye is interested in exploring the more social relationships at the personal level. This evident in both his recently published works, the short story *A Sense of Home* and the excerpts from his screenplay *A Long Way from Hollywood*. The first explores the mind of a child grappling with family relationships and understanding sexuality. In the story, a young boy tries to understand his and work out the relationship between his mother and the two men in her life—Mr. Quek and Mr. Heng. This leads him to make conclusions about who his "real" father is. These issues also leads him to ponder over relationships and their sexual outcomes. The published excerpts of the screenplay, on the otherhand, highlight cross-cultural relationships of a Malaysian male trying to land a movie role in the United States.

Going by Kee Thuan Chye's recent works, it would be reasonable to believe that his concerns in his creative works have changed significantly. There is little evidence of the "rebel with a cause" characteristics in them. His attention seems to have diverted to human and social issues at the personal level.

Kee Thuan Chye's first play, *1984, Here & Now* (1984) mocks the advent of censorship. Adapted from George Orwell's classic novel, *1984*, the play explores "Big Brotherdom" in Malaysia and finds that the human spirit is stronger and far more resilient than the cynical and manipulative power of mere politicking. In the play, Kee Thuan Chye creates the awarenesses of Malaysia as a fractured multiracial society. *1984, Here & Now* is a play which normally would have transformed itself into something else by self-censorship in the hands of a less principled writer.

Wiran, the protagonist, is jaded, cynical, but falls in love with a woman who could betray him. He struggles to come to terms with himself and his inability to accept others. Together with Jumon and Shadrin who betray him in the end, Wiran tries to find the answer to all the injustice and weakness in the multiracial society that is not integrated. Wiran meets Yone and discovers his vulnerability when he falls in love with her. He confronts the injustice, hears of a possible solution offered by a movement for a new Brotherhood. He joins in the hope that they might have the answers to the problems of society. The characters walk around with placards demanding truth, justice and freedom of expression which is suicidal in a police state. *1984, Here & Now* does not offer any resolution. Kee Thuan Chye allows the audience to decide on the resolution.

In *The Big Purge* (1987) Kee Thuan Chye continued the intense interrogation of government policy in a no-holds-barred manner that courted censorship. It is inspired by real events in 1987 when the Malaysian Government used powers invested in the International Security Act (ISA), and made many political arrests to curb extremism and ethnic tension. The play depicts Malaysians caught in the middle of these developments in Malaysian politics. Five people, a Malay couple Junid and Mazlina, and a Chinese married couple Wei Liang and his wife Joan, and the common friend of all, Ravindran, an Indian, are the central characters in the play. Injustice and tragedy stalk the characters; Joan loses her child in a racial stampede, extremists accuse Wei Liang and Mazlina of *khalwat* or close proximity (a punishable offence in Islamic law) causing Junid to accuse both of betraying him, while Ravindran loses heart and plans to migrate to Australia. *The Big Purge* depicts the fragile state of racial co-existence in Malaysia.

In *Birch* (1994), significant event in Malaysian history is interrogated. The historic event of the killing of the first British Resident to Perak, J.W.W. Birch is not new to Malaysian theatre in English. Before the staging of *Birch*, the Malaysian literary scene had already been introduced to it through K. S. Maniam's *Birch and the Rod*, and Lee Joo For's *The Happening in the Bungalow*. However, *Birch* is distinctly different in that the play refuses to be placed into a particular theatrical category.

The play based on a significant episode in Malaysian history; the killing of J. W. W. Birch, the first British Resident in colonial Malaya also depicts the power struggle between the feuding Malay chiefs in Perak. Subsequently, the play gives way to disarray, and the audience / readers suddenly realise they are watching a play in rehearsal. Shalini Teresa Fernandez (1995) says in Kee Thuan Chye's *Birch*, "Players shrug in and out of character at the drop of a hat, forcing the audience to change their focus constantly. The shifting locus of what is "theatrical" and what is "real" on the stage forces the viewers to assimilate with great visual impact the idea that all chronicles and reality are merely a matter of perception. *Birch* is by no means a historical play. It is a play more about the present than the past. It weaves together a bit of history and a lot of humour and irony, and gets to the heart of issues that concern Malaysians today. The play takes issue on the abuse of power, the pursuit of self-interest, the clash between Eastern and Western cultures, and the questionable role of history as a record of the truth.

In *Birch*, Kee Thuan Chye shows that one can never be sure about history, and of who is telling the truth because the characters in the play frequently break out of character and think "did this really happen in history?" These actions also throw the question open to the audience. The audience sits up and thinks "Oh yeah, maybe he's got a point there!" Hence, Kee Thuan Chye uses his medium (and technique) to convey the message that we cannot really trust history. The medium is the message. Inadvertently, the play also questions things like government's statements and newspaper reports. Wong Phui Nam (1984, n.p), says that "interspersions are deliberately introduced into the play for a functional purpose". He adds that "the achievement of the discourse which comes across to the understanding at many levels of meaning and tone, depends very much on Kee Thuan Chye using the device the actors speak out of their character" (n.p).

The effect of these techniques are quite indeterminate. Lloyd Fernando describes the play in this way:

> [Kee Thuan Chye] moves his audience from sombre contemplation of social realities of the time to sheer farce, and from there to modern political commentary, and back all over again. So what do we have? Perhaps a historical farce. Then again it may be a farcical history. Perhaps it is, instead, a dramatised seminar on the question: what is historical truth? But it could also be a holding up of a mirror to our own follies and tyrannies.

(1994, p. 1)

Kee Thuan Chye's writing style has changed somewhat since *1984, Here & Now*. It was then a very confrontational and direct, agitating for change. *Birch* on the hand, demonstrated a mellowing, subtleness not evident in his earlier plays. Kee Thuan Chye says of this:

> I've grown older and my world-view is a bit more different and I've learned certain things as well, so my approach would also change. It is inevitable in the development of any writer to pass through certain phases. When I wrote *1984, Here and Now*. I was young and angry but when I came to write *Birch*, I hoped I was more mature and able to see things on a broader perspective. I wasn't as didactic as I was in 1984—wanting to change people, tell people you should do this, you should do that. *Birch*, was more of presenting the situation and letting people decide for themselves.
>
> (cited in De Silva and Liging, 1995, p. 24)

Birch is an unpartisan of play. It tries to present various view points to the same issue. It is not didactic. It allows readers or audience to form their own conclusions. Techinically, *Birch* is by far the most dynamic of Kee Thuan Chye's plays. This is demonstrated by interesting techniques such as having the actors break out of character and address the audience or address some contemporary social issue while relating it to the play or the past. Such innovations work well in the context of the play.

As with *Birch*, Kee Thuan Chye's works always carry the signature of a "wicked and cogent satire of the political and social screnes afftecting all Malaysian wrapped up in a somewhat avantgarde absurdist presentation" (Fernandez, 1995, p. 11).

Kee Thuan Chye blends into his plays an English which Malaysians use daily. At the risk of his works being labelled inferior, Kee Thuan Chye has exploited so naturally the Malaysian variety of English in most of his works. The is evident even in his newspaper articles as shown below:

> De oder day, I went to see dis picture call Se Medan Jaya, and I tell you aah it is so stereotype, I dono wat to

say laa. The story like nutting to it, you know, like as though dey got no fresh idea.

(*NST*, 1984, p. 33)

Kee Thuan Chye promotes with pride such nativised use of language. His plays *1984, Here & Now* and *The Big Purge* have received international recognition as blunt and straight forward satire that ridicules the "corruption" of power in developing nations. *The Big Purge* was staged in Essex University in England, putting Malaysian Literature in the literary map of the world. These plays together with *Birch*, paved the way for open dialogues about issues related to race relations, national consciousness and identity, as well as in examining the role of politics in Malaysian life. His contribution is more in the direction of cultivating awareness among Malaysian audience particularly of the need to be less race conscious, and to be aware of the degree of political oppression and racial discrimination.

Birch is a kind of play that makes people take themselves less seriously; something that all Malaysians need to do. His work on *Birch* also contributes to Malaysian Literature by being unique in the sense that we seldom see plays which have multiple roles for the actors where the actors break out of characters. Currently, *Birch* is being used at local universities in Malaysia for the study of Malaysian Literature, and this indeed is a major contribution by Kee Thuan Chye.

11.3 Conclusion

Apart from his direct involvement in writing and theatre, Kee Thuan Chye's contribution to Malaysian literature is through great work he did while being Entertainment Editor and Literary Editor at the *New Straits Times*. Under his editorialship, the literary pages were the moving force behind many national literary activities and debates.

Kee Thuan Chye as a playwright, may be considered both foolish and courageous because of the unwavering stand he has taken in all his significant works thus far. He has taken liberties that would avert many other more established writers in calling into dialogue issues both sacred and taboo in the Malaysian social and political context. His open challenge of the establishment and of acceptable practices bear testimony to this. In much of his writing Kee Thuan Chye has exploited the "freedom" allowed his kind of thought to the limit. These present some of Kee Thuan Chye's contribution, not only as one of the protagonist in Malaysian literature, but also as a source of enlightenment to the general public on the stark realities of life in this country.

Bibliography

Primary texts

Kee, T. C. (1980). A figure forgotten in hours not of need. in *SARE 11*, (n.p). (Republished in 1988 in K. S. Maniam, and M. Shanmughalingham (eds.), *An anthology of Malaysian poetry*. Kuala Lumpur: Dewan Bahasa dan Pustaka.)

———. (1987). *1984 Here & Now*. Kuala Lumpur: Vintex Trading Company.

———. (1990, January–March). Once upon a sometime dream. *SARE 21*, (n.p). (Republished in 1991 in *Solidarity, 129*, (n.p)

———. (1990, January–March). Picture. *SARE, 21*, (n.p)

———. (1991). Tragic heroes suffer to be wise. *SARE, 23*, (n.p)

———. (1991). Moon over Manila. *SARE, 23*, (n.p).

———. (1991, January–March). Pieces of moon. *Solidarity, 129*, (n.p)

———. (1991, January–March). Once upon a sometime dream. *Solidarity, 129*, (n.p).

———. (1991, January–March). Mama's home. *Solidarity, 129*, (n.p)

———. (ed.). (1991). *Haunting the tiger and other stories*. Kuala Lumpur: Berita Publishing Sdn. Bhd.

———. (1994). *We could **** you, Mr. Birch*. Kuala Lumpur: Author.

Plays

1. *Oh, But I don't Want to Go, But I have to* (1974)
2. *Eyeballs, Leper and a Very Dead Soldier* (1977)
3. *The Situation of the Man Who Stabbed a Dummy or a Woman and was disarmed by the Members of the Club for a Reason Yet Obscure, If There was One* (1974)
4. *1984, Here & Now* (1984)
5. *The Big Purge* (1988)
6. *We Could**** You, Mr Birch* (1994)
7. *Old Doctors Never Fade Away*

Reviews & Critiques

Choo, L. L. (1994, June 23). Olahan baik Kee Thuan Chye. *Berita Harian*.

De Silva, M. & Liging, N. (1995). *The voice of the mute*. Unpublished interview wih Kee Thuan Chye. School of Language Studies and Linguistics, Faculty of Social Sciences and Humanities, UKM

Dorall, E. (1993, February 13). Prose of an unafraid basher. *New Starits Times*.

Fernandez, S. T. (1995, August 27). A truly Malaysian satire. *Sunday Star*.

Fernando, L. (1994, June 23). Review of the play *We could **** Mr. Birch*. [Review of the play *We could **** Mr. Birch*]. *New Straits Times*.

Wong, P. N. (1994, July 6). A multidimensional discourse in Birch. [Literary/Other cadences section]. *New Straits Times*.

Salleh ben Joned

12.0 Epigraph

Self-censorship is a universal disease, but I believe its local manifestation is quite peculiar, very "Malaysian" in an unflattering sense of the word. And what's more, it's becoming quite insidious. Those infected with this disease don't always realise it; even when they do, they try to pretend that it's unavoidable or justifiable. One can understand the self-censorship if the "integrity" of the writer's *periuk nasi* (rice bowl) is really at stake. But when it isn't and yet he still censors himself, one questions not so much his moral integrity as his intelligence. Basically, it's a question of perception—perception of what constitutes risks or dangers and the problem with our writers and literary middlemen. Ours is a sensitive country, and people involved in the business of writing are extremely sensitive people, not to things like stupidity, narrow-mindedness, corruption, threats to their freedom, but to alleged sensitivity of certain subjects.

—Salleh ben Joned,
As I Please
(1994, p. 52)

12.1 Introduction

Salleh ben Joned was born in Malacca in 1941. Son of a taxi driver, Salleh received his primary and secondary education in Malacca. He went on further studies in Australia where he became acquainted with two of Australia's great poets—James McAuley and A. D. Hope whose poetry Salleh greatly admires. After spending ten years in Australia for his first and M. A. degrees, Salleh returned to Malaysia and worked as a lecturer at the University of Malaya. He quit his position after ten years' of service and has since become a freelance writer.

Salleh is highly influenced by McAuley and Hope. McAuley was a radical poet and came from the generation of Australian men who drank heavily, told bawdy jokes and called a spade a spade (for which he was famous). Salleh attributes his interest in poetry to McAuley in *As I Please*:

> But it's Jim the teacher of literature and poet whom I want to recall in this essay in homage, though it is true that the public figure cannot be separated from the teacher and poet; in all the three roles he was distinguished by full-bodied convictions, by the firmness of his stand.
>
> (1994, p. 7)

Salleh, similarly, stands firm in his convictions about many things, as will be revealed in this chapter. He is not afraid of going beyond the parameters.

12.2 Discussion of works

Salleh is author of *Sajak-sajak Salleh: Poems Sacred and Profane* and a collection of essays aptly named *As I Please* to reflect both the quirky nature of their appearance in his column and the subject matter of these essays. One of Salleh's characteristics, which endears him to some and repulses others, is his penchant for testing the parameters. In his article "Testing the Parameter" in *As I Please* (1994, p. 51) he argues that the Malaysian censorship laws are "very stringent". As Cecil Rajendra laments in his poetry, the Internal Security Act forever plagues radical writers. Salleh ben Joned gets away with unsympathetic accounts of people and places because he "exploits the limited freedom that exists". As Salleh further explains:

> If self-censorship is bad for the general intellectual development of a country, it's worse for the development of its literature. I feel there is something about literature that makes self-censorship particularly bad for its health. Official censorship doesn't always have that effect, as the development of the literatures of Eastern European

countries during the time of the Communist dictatorships testified. But as it involves creative writers, this self-censorship can be so ingrained in certain areas of thinking and feeling (that involving religion, say, or race) that it no longer appears like self-censorship. It operates at the level of the unconscious, even before the imagination can produce the germ of an idea or perception. Such writers can only be pitied, because without realising it, they have betrayed their calling. Perhaps the prevalence of such writers is one explanation for the general predictability of our literature today.

(1994, pp. 52–3)

Thus Salleh experiments with parameters in many ways. His poems show his engagement with familiar things dealt in unfamiliar ways, making them unconventional, invigorating and sensuous. Adibah Amin (1987) aptly describes them as "rising above the barriers": which include his appreciation for women and what they represent, and the hypocrisy of "bumigeois" and etc. In his "afterword", Salleh confesses that his poetry celebrates "possibilities and variety". He abhors "conventions, concepts and slogans" (1987, p. 66).

In the bilingual 68-poem collection of *Poems Sacred and Profane*, Salleh exposes his multi-faceted persona. He explains the rationale behind the chosen title for his anthology:

What is allegedly "profane" could in fact be sacred, and vice versa. The line that is seen to separate the sacred and the profane can be a thin line. In fact that line does not exist at all if an act or an attitude is seen from the point of view that is *salih* or *soleh*, a Malay word of Arabic origin that is used in the title of the Malay version of this book. Saleh can mean a number of things: (a) pious (b) someone who comes and goes (c) odd.

(1987, n.p)

We find the whimsical Salleh (in *A Hymn to My Sarong*), the pensive *(Whence Does Love Come From)*, the lover of arts, and the wordsmith unafraid to wrestle with bereavement. But because Salleh mixes the sacred and the profane, he is seen as not representative of the Malay artist. Malaysians often refer to whites as "Mat Saleh". As Salleh himself says:

> Because of the values that inform my poems, and because I used to be married to two white women ...I am often called *Mat Saleh*. . . . Am I still a "Malay" or have I become a *Mat Saleh* of sorts? If I were asked such a question, my answer would be such questions do not mean anything to me. There are other questions that are more important and more meaningful.

(1987, p. 66)

In *Ria,* one of his favourite poems, triggered by the memory of his dead daughter, Salleh celebrates life and accepts death. The epigraph taken from the Chapter 16 of the Quran ". . . and we know what his soul whispereth to him, and We are nearer to him than the jugular vein" invites readers to understand two important things about Ria—that the speaker accepts the inevitability of his daughter's death, and that he celebrates the happy, albeit short memories she has given him. While many of Salleh's other poems may seem insensitive, ironic, and irrepressibly earthy, *Ria* is a moving poem recounting the verve and energy of a child:

> You were standing on the slope of the path,
> Your feet anchored to a mass of leaves
> Clinging damply to the earth.
> You saw me off with a sticky kiss,
> Sensing your moment in the slant of light,
> Your bewildered voice lisping a wish
> I couldn't hear

(1987, p. 1)

The overt use of fricative sounds show the tender feelings of a father compared to the hard guttural sounds of the medical officer informing the speaker of the death of his child—"your child is dead". Ria, nearer to the speaker than his own jugular vein shows the closeness between the father and daughter. Writing about her death becomes therapeutic:

> Now you are dead, I want to dream
> Your physicality
> Back into this house
> In which you hardly lived.
> Defiantly, I filled the rooms
> With your laughing faces, defiling
> The ritual of denial
> I'd been taught to observe.

                                                                    (1987, n.p)

Even though she is closer to him than his own jugular vein, her death would mean his death as well. But the father does not dwell on this. Instead, he rejects denying her death, although the pain of her death never totally disappears—"I sit here, my pen bleeding words/gripped by fingers bruised/from cutting your name/into sandstone. By speaking of her death and his anguish, he restores life to her—she will eternally be remembered in the pages of poetry. One is reminded of Shakespeare's *Sonnet 18* where the female lover is immortalised.

Poems which some may consider bordering profanities are those which celebrate sexual acts. *Obscenity* describes the passion of two lovers; the speaker expresses regret that the morning after normality resumes as his lover's "distant gnarled voice snarls across the crease" and the speaker himself is "spiritless" (1987, p. 8). The physicality of their intimacy is not extended after the act, which perhaps explains their alienation from each other—a relationship built on lust rather than love. Whatever the state of the relationship, Salleh stretches the parameters of Malaysian sensibilities, where one does not describe one's love-making sessions or refer to graphic details such as "the crumpled warmth of sheer white sheets / taints us with sudden staleness". Matters relating to bedrooms and what happens in there remains, to many Malaysians, private to the partners concerned.

Thus, Salleh throws caution to the winds. In his poems *The Woman Who Said No* and *The Woman who Said Yes*, he celebrates the wonders of sexual union of a man and a woman. In *The Woman Who Said No*, Salleh describes the birth of a prophet, even though the union that takes place may seem unholy:

> He was working in the clay when it came,
> This unseemly desire at the hour of dusk;
> To the nearest woman of his harem he went,
> His Quraysh eyes gleaming with inspired lust.

> (1987, p. 14)

The woman, however, rejects the man's advance and tells him to wash himself before bedding her: "Told to wash, to another woman he went, / taking with him the promise and the Light". This unholy union results in the conception of a child:

> Thus a prophet was conceived in the gust of lust
> Springing from the Omnipotent, earthy in its thrust.

In this poem, Salleh articulates his belief that little separates the sacred from profane. The woman who rejects her man has missed the opportunity to mother a child-prophet.

In another poem, a contrast to the woman who says no, Salleh draws a picture of an accommodating woman:

> Trembling with terror, he reached for her skirt;
> The echo of the fierce voice in the cave
> Still thundrered in the depths of his soul:

> "Cover me, Khatijah!" Devil or angel?
> The sweat of terror drowned his certainty.

"Get inside me! And you know for sure,"
He did—and terror burst into ecstasy.

The apparition withdrew with angelic tact,
His prophethood was confirmed in the act.

(1987, p. 15)

In this poem, the compliant woman provides love and warmth to the frightened man, which in turn gives the man courage to accept his prophethood. In the history of Prophet Muhammad, he was overcome with terror when an angel appeared before him and told him of his impending prophethood. He sought refuge in Khatijah but whether it was their conjugal act that calmed his nerves is probably conjecture on Salleh's part. What Salleh celebrates, rather, is the fact that a union between man and woman is a beautiful thing, a cause for celebration in the pages of Malaysian literature.

Salleh also tests the parameters with his perception of Malays. The fact that many Malays, he claims, see him as a Mat Salleh (a white) suggests that Salleh's sensibilities may be more influenced by his Western education. Salleh is unrelentless in his ironic portrayal of "bumigeoise"—a term he coins to show his aversion for hypocrite Malays. The poem *Harum Scarum* is printed in full to capture Salleh's views:

Drinking, gambling, lying, bribery,—
And all kinds of whoring too–
All of them perfectly okay.
And to hog it all's not taboo.

All sins of course; but nothing really
A trip to the Holy of Holies
Cannot fix for Eternity:
God blesses man's enterprise.
But that—that's different, untouchable!
We're Moslems, and terribly Malay.

Some things are just unmentionable;
The rest are okay if we pray.

We'll go the whole hog if we must
To redeem our pride as a race;
Like the giddy hare in a rut,
We'll *halal* everything save that.

It's hogwash what those swines say:
That we Bumis mount pig-a-back,
Like a pack of boars hacking our way
Up the slippery slope of success.

Our one dislike we have to keep
To preserve our identity;
So long as we hate pigs and pray,
We'll remain Moslem and Malay.

(1987, p. 34)

Salleh highlights the problems with a section of Malays who take pride in their race and yet indulge in things forbidden in religion such as drinking, gambling and promiscuity because they rationalise that at the end of the day they can perform the Haj and everything is forgiven. Preservation of the Malay identity is crucial to them but their understanding of that identity is shallow—as long as they "hate pigs and pray", they think themselves as authentic Malays. The phenomenon of sleeping partners in businesses where Malays use their names in registering businesses so that they may enjoy *Bumiputera* status, and yet their non-Malay partners do most of the work is also mentioned. Salleh calls this "pig-a-back" to emphasise the unscrupulous ways in which some Malay businessmen carry out their transactions. Salleh hints that these people are not Malays because they sell their Malay souls for material wealth. In short, people like them behave worse than the pigs they abhor.

In *Menage a Trois* Salleh again brings up the quandary that Malays have found themselves in whilst enjoying greater economic prosperity. Using the neologism "bumigeoise", to depict the relative wealth which Malays now enjoy, he highlights an example of the artificiality that mark their relationships. For example, the bored wife, says the speaker, is caught in a triangle relationship between the husband, TV heroes in the likes of J. R. or Bobby of American television series and food. When seen together with *Harum Scarum*, we cannot help noticing that Salleh is poking fun at the spiritual aridity of contemporary Malays.

It would be wrong, however, to suggest that all Malays are seen as hypocrites. In *The Balada of Mat Solo* or *Mat Solo's Last Stand*, Salleh describes the tragedy of Mat Solo, a Malay man driven to his death because of mental depression. Here we see a man caught in a psychological limbo, trapped between modernity as he stands "on the dizzy height of a monstrous power pylon" flicking his burning Lucky into the air, and tradition as he thrusts his kris into an innocent bystander. Mat Solo perceives himself as the victim whose manhood has been the insulted, and he reacts in the common tradition of many Malays pushed to react in the frenzy of the liver—he runs amok. In complete reversal to previous ironic portrayal of empty-headed "bumigeois", Mat Solo is depiated as a fallen hero whose death is regretabbly immature.

12.3 Conclusion

Salleh, with his magnetic pull towards controversy, is indisputably one of the finest poets in Malaysia. His bold approach in testing the parameters shows us a mind unable to censor itself. He articulates what most Malaysians already know about the cultural demography of Malaysia, but lacks the courage and the skill to pen them as Salleh does. While many writers doubt Salleh's sensitivities as typical of a Malay, the issues he articulates in most of his poems and essays show us that he is truly a son of the soil.

Bibliography

Primary Texts

Salleh ben Joned (1987). *Sajak sajak Saleh: Poems sacred and profane.* Kuala Lumpur: Teks Publishing.

———. (1994). *As I please: Selected writings 1975–1994.* London: Skoob Books Publishing Ltd.

———. (2002). *Sajak sajak Saleh: Poems sacred and profane.* Kuala Lumpur: Pustaka Cipta.

———. (2003). *Nothing is Sacred.* Petaling Jaya: Maya Press.

Secondary Texts

Alia Anreen. (2003, January 5). Unflinching collection. *Sunday Star.*

Adibah Amin. (1987). Rising above the barriers. (Reprinted in *Sajak-sajak Salleh,* pp. xi-xii, Salleh ben Joned, 2002, Kuala Lumpur: Pustaka Cipta)

Masjaliza Hamzah. (January 5, 2002). A poet's digressions. *Sunday Star.*

Sadna Saifuddin. (November 13, 2003). Sacredly Salleh. *New Straits Times.*

Emerging Voices

13.0 Epigraph

Unambiguously Malaysian, their creative drive is fuelled by the ambiguities inherent in being Malaysian. Theirs—again perhaps as a consequence of the determined Malaysian-ness that has pervaded this air since they first drew breath—is undoubtedly the most inclusive Malaysian identity of all time. Educated, alert and aware, they subsume within themselves the divisions that had held their forbears apart, and bear their elaborately intertwined identities with grace in a wider world.

> —Rehman Rashid on the New Economy,
> post-1969 generation of young Malaysians in the
> foreword to *Generation* (1997, p. xxii)

13.1 Introduction

The twelve writers we have looked at are the established voices of Malaysian creative writing in English. Their published works, as Amir Muhammad puts it in the foreword to *Silverfish New Writing 1* (2001), "constitutes a real sense of tradition or oeuvre". Yet there are so many other voices that need to be considered if a truer appraisal of Malaysian literature in English is to be made. New writers, those born in the 1960s and 1970s and those not-so-young but newly published in the 1990s and after, will feature prominently in this chapter. The former are the young Malaysians Rehman Rashid refers to in the epigraph above—the generation shaped "by twenty years of one of the worlds most assiduous exercises in socio-economic engineering". But the chapter also acknowledges new voices who are older Malaysians, writers who added their stories to the corpus even as the younger, media savvy ones began their creative efforts. Placed together in all their variety, these new writings and new voices must surely provide an endless array of perspectives of the country. The focus will be on prose, fiction and plays since there is yet to appear new poetic voices who have written consistently or published their own anthology or anthologies.

This chapter thus provides an introduction of the 1990s to the present, and perhaps some insights into the new writings. It will not be an exhaustive survey but will foreground those writers who have established continuity and credibility in their creative writing. First-time published writers and a number of unpublished winners of competitions will be referred to because of the exciting possibilities of their creativity. The general approach will be similar to that of the other chapters, discussion of the thematic concerns against the context of social, political, linguistic, literary, economic developments and/or global events. Space constraints do not allow for much in-depth discussion. However, it is hoped important aspects of the works, which are highlighted will lead the way towards further reading and research. A selected bibliography for some of the writers is given at the end of the chapter.

The 1980s and 1990s are generally seen as decades of a positive change in attitude towards English. The national language policy of the 1970s, which had marginalised English was revised in the early 1980s. English was recognised as the global language for trade and technology. Through various government initiated strategies and policies, the relevance and necessity of mastering English was reinstated. The resulting resurgence in creative writing in English began in the early 1990s when we note the appearance of new names, writers if short stories, one-act plays, novels and plays for production. They would appear repeatedly in the ensuing years in newspapers, magazines, anthologies, theatre and on television.

14.3 Discussion of works
Much of the interest in matters literary and creative writing in the early 1990s was due in no small measure to the *New Straits Times*. It is to this that we now turn for some idea of the context, which gave

the opportunity for the first tentative steps towards a slow but steady development of creative writing in English. This was the literary section helmed by Kee Thuan Chye, two pages devoted to matters literary, ranging from Shakespeare to Malaysian writing, pre- and post-publicity for literature conferences and conference papers. At the heart of it was Wong Phui Nam's weekly "Literary Cadences"— perceptive, well-researched, thought-provoking discussions on a range of topics, almost all directly or implicitly linked with the local literary scene. The literary page was the site of a number of literary competitions. The *NST*-Shell Short Story Competition of 1989–1990 successfully set the literary ball rolling and in 1991, *Haunting the Tiger and Other Stories* (the collection of winning entries) was published with Kee Thuan Chye as editor. A Malaysian consciousness is apparent in these stories. We see a Malaysian identity not only in the characters and local details but also in the nature of the conflicts. Whilst there are clear attempts at presenting Malaysian English, the most significant aspect of these stories is the portrayal not just of various racial groups but of interactions and therefore, meaningful contact between them. The quest for the evolving of a Malaysian consciousness and the crafting of the short story form continued with two more *NST*-Shell competitions in 1991 and 1992. These garnered winners and short-listed entrants, some of whom would go on to produce more later: Mohammad Aziz Salim, Wong Ming Fook, Mallika Vasugi, Chuah Guat Eng, Marie Gerrine-Louis, Syed Adam Aljafri.

Established writers Syed Alwi (*I Remember the Rest House*), Lloyd Fernando (*Passage to Malaya*) and Edward Dorall (*The Death of the Old Man*) were the winners of the *NST*-Esso Playwriting Competition in 1993. K.S. Manian and Ghulam Sarwan Yusof (active in the 1970s) were consolation prize winners. Although no other competitions followed, Malaysian theatre in English would begin to expand at about this time and reference to some of the new playwrights will be made later.

Perhaps the most disappointing in terms of immediate or long-term development arising from increased activity and production is that of the *NST*-Shell Poetry Competition I and II (1993 and 1995). Of the new voices garnered from prize winners, Leonard Jeyam and Dina Zaman, continue to be in the public eye. Whilst the novel, short story and play scenarios appear to be thriving, there was a paucity of poetry publications in the 1990s. Bernice Chauly's *Going There and Coming Back* was published in 1997; one of ten creative books in the Rhino Press, Black and White series. These are poems derived from personal experiences—feelings for a lover, a family member, for a baby lost, for "unfulfilled memories" of a Chinese childhood. Chauly herself is now active in theatre, and is at present involved in playwriting and a memoir of her Ipoh childhood days. Perhaps the most engaging new poetry is from Charlene Rajendran's *Mangosteen Crumble* (1999). The title for the collection of poems aptly captures the multicultural diversity, interwining, blending and contradictions of the Malaysian context. The writer draws from the mixed bag of cultural and literary heritage she has inherited. As a Malaysian Indian professional, knowledgeable about Asian ways and attuned to Western mores and lifestyle, Charlene Rajendran voices her thoughts on our problems large and small, drawing on the smells, tastes, sights and sounds around us. As actor and teacher of language and literature, she endows her poems with variations of rhythm that are as pleasing to utter as they are to listen.

Whilst there is interest and passionate commitment to poetry (for example there is a poetry "zine" called *Poetika*), this is confined to small groups of people. Poetry publishing, for the writer as much as for the publishers, but for differing reasons, seems to be a domain few dare to enter.

The 1990s was a decade of anthologies of short stories and of first-time novels. Many of these were self-published, financed by the writers themselves. It was also a time when creative writing by women proliferated. Another feature was the contribution, to the corpus, of the writers of the Malaysian diaspora. Postcolonial studies, the study of contact literature of non-native speakers of English, cultural studies and comparative literature helped provide the infrastructure for these new works, making access to them not only fitting but also necessary. The symbiotic set-up was all the more enhanced with new works by established writers (K. S. Maniam, Wong Phui Nam), new issues of old classics and anthologies of criticism and creative work in Skoob Books' *Pacifica Anthology No.1* and 2. Perhaps the most significant feature was that for the first time there was truly a Malaysian racial spread of writers. Not only were Malays writing, there were also writers from East Malaysia, and also a truly varied (and typically) Malaysian spectrum of writers of mixed parentage or ancestry. With this came a shift away from earlier concerns of the predominantly Chinese and Indian writers in English. Problems of migrant displacement and alienation, issues of "rootlessness" and loss of identity, lack of racial harmony—these continued to be foregrounded, particularly by the established writers. However, newer concerns, no less political in nature, began to appear. A wide range of issues connected to modernisation, westernisation and nation-building emerged. As if to "fix" these within a Malaysian consciousness and context, these thematic concerns were rendered in a variety of nativisation of the English language. Whilst dialogues provided the most obvious channel for "Malaysianisms", there was a higher-level nativisation in the form and structure of the works and in the metaphors, images, rhetoric and discourse of the narratives. It is to these writers and their works that we now turn.

Kris Jitab's *Tales From a Headhunter* (1991) are comic-ironic stories of self-deception, of rejected love and greed, old subjects set in rural Sarawak, and fleshed out through concerns specific to the place; the strong hold of tradition, superstition and magic in the face of modernity, the colonial and colonised mind-set of the people.

Syed Adam Aljafri, one of the winners of the *NST*-Shell Short Story Competition 1 for *The Matsumoto Light Horse Artillery* went on to produce two short story collections: *Ollies' Search for Golden Hope and Other Stories* (1992) and *Reminiscences: A Collection of Short Stories* (1997). His stories revolve around issues and conflicts of contemporary Malaysia and its new middle-class with its corporate values, elitist, Anglophile tendencies; modernity and nationalism and intercultural and inter-racial relations. An ironic tone and the twist at the end of the tale, often connected with death, are familiar aspects of his work. He passed away in 1994.

In 1993, Che Husna Azhari's semi-autobiographical *Melor in Perspective* was published. Originally put together as a collection titled *Kelantan Tales*, these eight storiess are now preceded by an essay on the history of the "village-town" of Melor (a microcosm of Kelantan life) covering topics such as "Kaum Muda-Kaum Tua" "Women in Melor Politics" and etc. The sociological interest of Che Husna's stories is clearly set with the writer explaining in her preface that "memory of the nuances and peculiarities that make up the whole social spectrum in my stories can be explained by the essays".

The narrative voice in these stories, as in the second collection of stories of her childhood, *Rambutan Tales* (1993) is that of an educated bilingual Malay professional woman. The tone is humorous, one of affectionate irony. The stories are communicated in an inclusive, conversational manner reminiscent of the oral tells of the *Tok Selampit* of Kelantan. The Malaysian bilingual's creativity in nativising English has one of its most innovative and liberal examples in Che Husna's discourse. The informal spoken style of the (Western) educated Malay bilingual is adopted for both narrator/author's voice as well as in the dialogues of the Melor personalities. This means a wide spectrum of village characters (who in real life would speak Kelantanese Malay) are given to speaking-like urban bilinguals, deftly and humorously switching codes and adjusting grammatical niceties. Unlike the fictional creations of other writers whose dialogues are riddled by Manglish and mother-tongue interference, Che Husna's charming rice seller or village hit-man are free from fossilised grammatical errors! Che Husna's various linguistic innovations (a number of references on this aspect of her work are cited in the bibliography) are carried a step further in a collection of poems *Puisi Ambo* (*My Poems*). Of particular interest to Malaysian literature in English are two sets of poems under the subheading "Puisi Dwibahasa" and "Poyengs in Kelantan Inglishy."

Unlike Che Husna, Chuah Guat Eng in *Echoes of Silence* (1994) steers clear of nativisation except for the touch of local Malaysian Chinese to add linguistic colour but more importantly, to highlight the protagonist Ai-Lian's sense of distance and displacement from her own people and place of birth. Like Che Husna, she is also self-published. Chuah takes the ingredients of a mystery thriller then subverts the normal pattern of the genre's development by leaving the resolution not only to twenty years later, but to a nullifying of the need for punishment. Right and wrong, guilt and innocence, racial misconceptions as well as the importance of love and honest communication are some of the subjects explored. The historic frame of the novel spans the Malaya of the 1940s to 1990s, with events tracking back and forth allowing the reader to make the interconnections. More importantly, it provides a history of the country as seen through the events (and the "silences") Ai-Lian ("a wandering Chinese Malaysian") experiences. The novel is truly Malaysian in the breadth of history it provides, its spread of multiracial postcolonial Malaysians, its implicit message of the interconnectedness of our lives through a history shared and in the way it draws from the religious-cultural trove. Two Buddhist discourses, the Diamond Sutra and the Heart Sutra inform the overall plot and structure of this story, a Malaysian seeking her "enlightenment".

The questions related to identity in postcolonial Malaysia could be a useful way of looking at many of the novels written in the 1990s. Chuah presents the displacement of the Western educated middle class Chinese woman, and clearly suggests a happy closure in her ability to cross cultural boundaries—by virtue of those very aspects that previously alienated her. Marie Gerrine-Louis in *The Road to Chandibole* (1994) (again a woman-centred novel) also uses the historical frame to tell the story of Saraswathy who survives class and gender discrimination of life in the estate. Saraswathy's survival and her marriage to Tjun King suggest not only the importance of grit and strength of character but the need to transcend caste, racial and social barriers. Although the protagonist is an Indian male in the second novel *Junos* (1995), there is a similar emphasis on the fearless fight for survival and happiness based on values that rise above material gain and standing.

Stories of strong women who survive and overcome obstacles to achieve self-fulfilment whether material or otherwise is also taken up by two Malaysian-born writers who now reside overseas. In the early 1990s, Beth Yahp (based in Australia) wrote *The Crocodile Fury* (1992). A ghost-chasing grandmother tells the story of her early days as a servant in a rich man's mansion and of her adopted daughter, to a granddaughter (the narrator of the story). Superstition, myth and historical detail are woven into this story of Chinese women.

More recently, the empowering stories of mothers and grandmothers, have been harnessed for another woman-centred story *The Rice Mother* by Rani Manicka who lives in England. This is the story of Lakshmi who comes to Malaya from Ceylon at the age of fourteen as a child bride. The story unfolds from multiple points of view of her children, her grandchildren and great grandchild, Nisha, the one who records all the stories. The Japanese occupation is central to the story because this is when Lakshmi's strength of character, indeed her almost inhuman, alienating protectiveness is shown. To the end, she is fierce and logical, and this is the legacy she leaves to the women who come after her. There is a wealth of physical details of people, and the sights and sounds of Malaya and Malaysia. The suffering caused by the Japanese on the local people is the context for Lakshmi's constant battle with obstacles. The backdrop also consists of strange exotic practices, snake charmer secrets and powers, dark family secrets and mysterious unravellings, and destructive charms and potions in modern day Malaysia.

Karim Raslan's expose of the materialistic, self-serving ways of upper class Malays is completely different from the affectionate, almost idyllic portrayals of Che Husna Azhari's Kelantan Malays. The quaint, self-sufficient, wholly Malay setting of Melor morphs into Malaysia's urban, international residential communities. In Karim's stories the stance and tone is that of the inside-outsider, and the irony is often caustic and sharp. What comes across is a wide cross-section of plastic corporate heads, squabbling siblings, well-heeled glitterati and angst- ridden yuppies, all engaged in the worship of the good life for themselves, for their family status and connections and all for public consumption. It is in these conditions that Karim probes into secrets and quirky silences of the pillars of society. Read together with his essays on Malaysian politics and society, Karim's short stories are the fictional manifestations of old and new maladies that plague contemporary Malaysia and the new Malays. They provide a rich resource for cultural studies and readings with reference to nationhood and nation building. The consistent emphasis on the barren posturing of upper and middle class Malay life places him (he certainly qualifies age wise) together with those young Malaysians who foreground contemporary social issues, such as poverty, sexual discrimination and greed. Certainly, the "sensual and shocking" aspect of Karim's writing is seen in a good number of the stories and the single collection of poems by Bernice Chauly mentioned earlier, and in the writing of Dina Zaman.

The ten books published by the Rhino Press under the Black and White eries (1997) consist of six collections of short stories, a fantasy, a film script, a collection of poems and a human rights account of the Indonesia-East Timor conflict. There are a variety of styles, even within the short-story genre in which the focus is on those on the fringes of society—"dirty, menial and degenerate", and on women, rich and poor battling with patriarchy and tradition. The old preoccupation with migrant "rootlessness" and alienation, of racial identity and disharmony now make way for psychological, emotional, and social dislocations that arise out of conflicts of modern life. Although the Black and Whites series was the only Rhino Press publication, it served to bring many unknowns or previous literary competition winners to public attention. Although styles differed, there was a shared concern to highlight conflicts, personal or of larger import, in an honest and accessible manner. These were the new Malaysians whose education had been "laden with the imperatives of the New Economic Policy, Malaysia's first global generation, born and raised for the Information Age" (Rehman, foreword to *Generation*, 1997, p. xxi). In their settings, the stories encapsulate the multicultural scenario of the novels and short stories of the 1990s. In their ironic perspective they take up the critical, thought-provoking stance of writers such as Kee Thuan Chye, Salleh ben Joned, and of Rehman Rashid in *The Malaysian Journey* (1993).

The late 1990s saw a flurry of creative publications. Ellina Abdul Majid's self-published *Perhaps in Paradise* (1997) and *Khairunnissa, A Good Woman* (1998) are woman/family-centred stories of growing up and gaining self-knowledge amidst, and in spite of, unstable and disruptive family relations.

The multicultural diversity of modern day Malaysia finds a different tack in Tunku Halim's (based in Australia) horror fiction. These are the novel *Dark Demon Rising* (1997) and two collections of short stories *The Rape of Martha Yeoh and other Chilling Stories* (1997) and *Vermillion Eye* (2000). He taps into the Malaysian horror chest of *pontianaks* and assorted ghosts for every kind of human evil and weakness. The settings range from the corporate corridors of money and power to the jungles of war-torn Malaya. The world of devilry, tampering with the natural order of things and crime is always balanced with that of normalcy and spiritual strength and order. In the end, order is established, as with *Dark Demon Rising*, when the protagonist returns to the village and his true love. Even if there is no closure as such, the message is clear: crime and consorting with dark forces do not pay.

Tapping into another aspect of Malaysia's cultural heritage, Uma Mahadevan's *The Twice Born* (1998) reaches into her ethnic past and sets her story in the Indus valley 1500 B.C. The spiritual awakening of a young priest has a parallel in the story of a Ceylonese psychiatrist in modern day Malaysia who has to treat an autistic child. Here is a story with no social axe to grind other than the writer's need to write and publish her own book and indulge in her knowledge of ancient Indian history, astrology, archaeology and medicine, to name a few. Who is to say that the novel is not as relevant as those with obvious social issues? It is an example of creativity that helps to remind us who are perpetually engaged in nation-building, of the need to know and draw from the shared wisdom of our diverse peoples.

There was a time, particularly in the 1970s and 1980s, when collectively, samplings of Malaysian writing in English appeared more often in overseas journals and publications than in those at home. The publication of the *Skoob Pacifica Anthologies 1 & 2* (1993 and 1994 respectively) made a difference because the contents devoted a substantial sub-section to creative writings and critical articles. For prose writing at any rate, beginning with the late 1990s, there have been quite a few collections of short stories. In 1998, Mohammad A. Quayum put together a selection of short stories *In Blue Silk Girdle*. In 2001, Silverfish Books published *Silverfish New Writing I* followed by the second one in 2002. The latest to appear is

Nineteen (2003), a collection of stories by women, seven of which are by Malaysians. In 2002, *The Merlion and Hibiscus* was published by Mohammad A. Quayum with a selection of Malaysian and Singaporean short stories. The selection includes recent and not-so-recent works and writers, for example Che Husna Azhari, M. Shanmughalingam, Chuah Guat Eng and Karim Raslan. The latest addition is *Petals of Hibiscus: A Representative Anthology of Malaysian Literature in English* edited by Mohammad A. Quayum (2003). The selections for fiction, poetry and drama consist of works by established and new writers.

An overarching concern of many of the stories, particularly the new material in the Silverfish books, is the modernisation of Malaysia and with this the socio-cultural, economic, political change and conflicts, big and small, humorous or with tragic consequence, that affect and dislocate the people. Acute loneliness, psychological and emotional drifting apart, disillusionments over material priorities, urban life and love with its various forms of cruelties are the various aspects of modern life to be found in these stories. The search for solace, refuge, consolation takes many forms. There are possibilities of harmony and self-knowledge. More often than not, there is tragedy or an open-endedness, and ambiguity that is full of foreboding. The use of shifting perspectives and effective structuring can be seen in one of *The Best of New Writing 1*, S. Chinniah's *Tamarind Tree*. The story relates to the events on the last day of Uncle Das who torches himself under the Tamarind tree. The omniscient narrator acquaints us with the man's utter isolation and deep weariness with life. The horror of the torching and the lack of feeling shown by the wife and neighbours are poignantly related by a friend of Das' daughter who recollects what she saw as a ten-year-old that fateful day. The tragic vignette of the superficialities of the contemporary Malaysian life is only partly muted in the end by the love and kindness between the two little girls.

Four years into the new century, the opportunity for consideration of manuscripts, and for publishing is better than it has ever been. Perhaps in the not too distant future, promising Malaysian writers will have the same kind of opportunities as Malaysian-born Rani Manicka, whose first novel *The Rice Mother* (2002) is published by Hodder & Stoughton.

After the doldrums of the 1970s, a slow restarting in the mid-1980s, theatre in English saw a steady revival in the 1990s, with accelerated activity in the second half of the decade and into the new. Theatre companies such as The Actors Studio Theatre and Five Arts have played crucial roles not only in ensuring a constant flow of presentations, but in promoting talent in script writing and acting through various projects. Plays performed ranged over a variety of local and imported fare. These included plays by Ramli Ibrahim, Kee Thuan Chye, Syed Alwi, Huzir Sulaiman and Jit Murad. There was a revival of Edward Dorall's *A Tiger Is Loose in Our Community* in the late 1990s.

The Actors Studio Theatre project, the Malaysian Playwright series (2002) produced *Sweet Nothing* by Gavin Yap, *Stories for Amah* by Mark de Silva and *A Goldfish Tale* by Choong Chi-Ren. Before that, the Studio's Young Writers Workshop Project (2001) presented *Reports of Our Deaths Have Been Greatly Exaggerated*. In 2003, Five Arts presented *7-Ten*, a set of seven 10-minute plays written by young Malaysians. Although some of the plays mentioned above have scripts that have been published, Malaysian drama in English as "published texts" lags behind the volume and variety of Malaysian theatre productions. This is a loss to those interested in contemporary Malaysian drama; for academia, it has meant a smaller corpus of drama texts for critical analysis and discussion.

In the early 1990s, Ramli Ibrahim's *In The Name of Love: A Play in Three Flushes* was added to the small number of existing Malaysian plays in English. He wrote the plays (originally in Malay) as a vehicle for the talents of Malaysian actor Sabera Shaik. With dance elements woven into each of the three "flushes", the plays showcase three contemporary women of different races. The love and loss they have experienced at the personal level parallel the cultural and social concerns of Malaysia, past, present and future. Whilst Sarasa humorously expresses the self-delusions of mothers who live out their ambitions through their children, Mak Su is a poignant revelation of the loneliness, yet acceptance, of a once-feted Mak Yong dancer who can look forward to neither reward nor recognition for her art. The plays have proven to have long shelf lives and the last performance of Mak Su and Sarasa was in March 2003.

Of the Rhino Press' Black and White series (1997), there was only one play, Dain Said's *Surabaya Johnny*. It is derived from a short film of the same name conceptualised and directed by the writer himself. The play is about a streetwise petty hoodlum as much a villain as a victim of society. The specific setting is Surabaya but the context is Indonesia before, and during the 1965 coup. In this play based on a fictional character and interlaced with discourse and documentary footage from "official sources", Dain explores the concoction of truth, the legitimising of that version of history deemed appropriate by those in power. He calls his film a "mockumentary" (1997, p. 13).

In *Silverfish New Writing 1*, there are two plays, Huzir Sulaiman's *Election Day* (to be discussed later) an extract from Five Arts Centre and Akshen's production of *Lebih Kecoh* and lastly an extract from a screenplay-in-progress *The Pretenders*.

Lebih Kecoh is ironic and humorous, totally Malaysian in the issues raised and in the language. Central to the play is the establishments' perception that young Malaysians do not understand the real significance of *Merdeka*. Then in a number of specific scenes, the young Malaysians (the actors) proceed to give their personal views or play out their roles pertaining to specific historical times the early days, the Japanese Occupation, colonial times, *Merdeka*, and the race riots of 1969. The play's central premise is that "all knowledge is constructed" or as Kee Thuan Chye puts it "We are all recipients of manipulated truth and are manipulators ourselves" (cited in R. Yeo's introduction to *We Could **** You Mr.Birch*, 1995, p. 14). Indeed the extract is reminiscent of Kee's play in its use of modern technical devices: the voice over, non-linear progress, real actors as characters and as Malaysian/historical figures speaking out of role; references to contemporary personalities and personal friends. Past and present fuse to reiterate the fact that post-mortems of any event are based on a particular version of truth or a contribution of different truths. The play balances the ignorance of the young actors about the past especially in relation to the significance of this or that, with the friendly, youthful warmth and honesty of these young Malaysians who have no hang ups about ethnic differences and keeping quiet about sensitive issues.

Huzir Sulaiman's scripts for plays have now been published in *Eight Plays* (2002). His plays are comic-ironic exposés of uniquely Malaysian illusions and delusions, prejudices and mindsets; his characters, a spread of moralistic sanctimonious, egocentric hypocrites, to intelligent, loving, kind individuals who live their lives with quiet dignity. Then there is the linguistic *rojak* that is "Malaysian English". This humorously captures the nuances of class, ethnic group and age perfectly, in a variety of exchanges that are one-tracked, self-absorbed, at cross-purposes (as in *Election Day* and *Atomic Jaya*), or reveal the depth of caring and love as in *The Four Sisters Fernandez*. Yet the language can also move from the mundane and hilarious to the lyrical and densely metaphoric.

The emotional and cultural conflicts at the personal level suggest the inconsistencies at the political, cultural and social levels in the country. In *Occupation*, an account of a touching love story sets off a train of thoughts for the interviewer and her modern-day problems. In *Notes on Life and Love and Painting*, we accept the protagonists' showy and elaborate oral defence of their stand because their sarcasm, and digs at our pretensions and egocentricities are totally justified.

The array of characters from likeable, thinking ones to (the larger number) of noisy know-alls and dim-witted decision-makers lends itself well to discussing Huzir Sulaiman's plays against the traditional characters of Greek drama. There are the *alazons* or impostors who are unaware and deluded, the *eirons* or self-deprecators and the buffoons (*bomolochoi*). *Eirons* are survivors because they are self-aware. Thus, in Huzir's plays, the deluded, inconsistent society will continue (the "humorous" society of Greek drama) but there will always be *eirons*, small stable points within the flux and noise of the Malaysian society. For at the heart of Huzir's plays is the importance of "kindness... that love must beat fear" (*Notes on Life and Love and Painting*) of, "loving" and "being loved"(*Occupation*) or, as it's put in *Hip Hopera*: "Long may [love] reign over all our dimensions."

There have been many outstanding scripts by Malaysians in the past few years. The most outstanding are Jit Murad's *Gold Rrain and Hailstones* staged in 1993, *Visits* (2002), *Spilt Gravy on Rice* (2002), and Yasmin Yaacob's *A Flight Delayed*. None of these have been published. With the Cameronian Arts Award which began in 2003, it is hoped that the support for Malaysian theatre will see an increase in the number of published scripts from writers such as Bernice Chauly, Mira Mustafa, Mark de Silva and others. It is perhaps in drama, more than any other genre that the rich multiplicity of culture and cultural traditions can be given life and immediacy. Huzir Sulaiman's plays prove that Malaysians can be politically provocative in their writing. When local theatre in English is more accessible and less confined to the urban capital, then Malaysian drama can entertain as well as "educate" more Malaysians to cross boundaries.

There is another category of Malaysian writing that needs to be mentioned. These are the memoirs/autobiographies, collections of essays and journalistic writings. Rehman Rashid's *A Malaysian Journey* (1993), Chong Sheau Ching's *Stories for My Mother* (2001), Amir Muhammad, Karim Raslan and Sheryll Stothard's *Generation* (1998), Karim Raslan's *Ceritalah! 1 and 2* (1996 and 2002 respectively), and Marina Mahathir's *In Liberal Doses* (1997) are some of the main examples. These works provide various perspectives on Malaysia and its people. These writings provide the socio-political and economic "reality" segments for our readings of the creative works. A critical appreciation of Lloyd Fernandez's two novels for example, with their emphasis on racial relations and May 1969, would be greatly enhanced by a reading of Rehman Rashid's *A Malaysian Journey.*

13.3 Conclusion

These then are some of the emerging voices on the Malaysia Literature in English wavelength. The corpus may seem small compared to that from Indian writers or even Singapore, but volume alone is not the most important criteria for measuring the well being of the enterprise. So long as there is healthy continuity, there will always be new additions to talk of and to discuss: the new against the old, the fiction against the non-fiction, the changes and permutations in style and focus. In short, the literature will be given the chance to grow, establishing not only a stronger Malaysian identity but also a global, post-national presence. Mulaikka Hijjas, Jerome Kugan, Mallika Vasugi, Rahel Joseph, M. Shanmughalingham, Noraini Md. Yusof, Nor Faridah Abdul Manaf, Dina Zaman, Leonard Jeyam, Ridzwan Othman and Saffura Chinniah to name just some of the published writers, will no doubt continue to write. There are others waiting in the wings such as M.K. Hew, Prabhaharan Rajendra and Muhammad Muzhafar Mohd. Mukhtar. Given the developments of the 1990s and the new century, it seems natural to believe that Malaysian writing in English can entertain and instruct with the many worlds to it offers. In adding their voice to Malaysian literature in English the writers are fulfilling Frantz Fanon's requirement for natural consciousness, that is to "work and fight with the same rhythm as the people to construct the future and to prepare the ground where vigorous shoots are already springing up" (1990, p. 222).

Bibliography

Primary Texts: Fiction, Drama, Poetry and Anthologies.

Amir Muhammad. (ed.). (2001). *Silverfish new writing 1*. Kuala Lumpur: Silverfish Books.

Aziz Salim. (1997). *A stroll through the other forest*. Petaling Jaya: Rhino Press.

Chauly, B. (1997). *Going there and coming back*. Petaling Jaya: Rhino Press.

Che Husna Azhari. (1993). *Melor in perspective*. Bangi, Selangor: Furada Publishing House.

———. (1993). *Rambutan orchard*. Bangi, Selangor: Furada Publishing House.

———. (1996). *Puisi ambo*. Bangi, Selangor: Furada Publishing House.

Comber, L. (ed.). (1991). *Prize winning Asian fiction*. Singapore: Times Books International.

Dain Said. (1997). *Surabaya Johnny*. Petaling Jaya: Rhino Press.

Dina Zaman. (1997). *Night & day*. Petaling Jaya: Rhino Press.

Ellina Abdul Majid. (1997). *Perhaps in paradise*. Kuala Lumpur: The Written Word.

———. (1998). *Khairunnissa, a good woman*. Kuala Lumpur: The Written Word.

Govindarajoo, M. V. (April 6, 2002). The graduation. *New Straits Times* [Life & Times section] (p. 6).

Gunnel, M. (1997). *Mother material*. Petaling Jaya: Rhino Press

Huzir Sulaiman. (2002). *Eight plays*. Kuala Lumpur: Silverfish Books.

Jit Murad. (1997). *2 things*. Petaling Jaya: Rhino Press.

Jitab, K. (1991). *Tales from a headhunter*. Singapore: Times Editions Pte. Ltd.

Joseph, R. (1997). *Beginnings*. Petaling Jaya. Rhino Press.

Kamal Bamadhaj & Nadia Bamadhaj. (1997). *Aksi write*. Petaling Jaya: Rhino Press.

Karim Raslan. (1998). *Heroes and other stories*. Singapore: Times Books International.

Kee, T. C. (ed.). (1991). *Haunting the tiger and other stories*. Kuala Lumpur: Berita Publishing Sdn.Bhd.

————. (ed.). (1991). *We could **** you, Mr. Birch* (Revised edition). Kuala Lumpur: Author

Lau, J. (ed.). (2003). *Nineteen: A collection of stories by women*. Kuala Lumpur: Silverfish Books.

Louis, M. G. (1994). *The road to Chandibole*. Singapore: Heinemann Asia.

Louis, M. G. (1995). *Junos*. Singapore: Heinemann Asia.

Mahendran, U. (1998). *The twice born*. Kuala Lumpur: Platinum Press.

Manicka, R. (2002). *The rice mother*. London: Hodder & Stoughton.

Mira Mustaffa. (1997). *Speak louder! darling*. Petaling Jaya: Rhino Press.

Quayum, M. A. (ed.). (1998). *In blue silk girdle*. Kuala Lumpur: Universiti Putra Press.

Mukerjee, D. et. al. (2002). *The merlion and the hibiscus: Contemporary short stories from Singapore and Malaysia*. New Delhi: Penguin Books.

Nandan, S. (ed.). (2002). *Silverfish New Writing 2*. Kuala Lumpur: Silverfish Books.

Ooi, Y. M. (1988). *The flame tree*. London: Hodder & Stoughton.

Ridzwan Othman. (April 17, 2002). Homemade explosive. *New Straits Times* [Life & Times section], (p. 7).

Rajendran, C. (2000). *Mangosteen crumble*. Kuala Lumpur: Team East.

Rehman Rashid. (1993). *A Malaysian journey*. Petaling Jaya: Author.

Saffura Chinniah. (April 3, 2002). Sashay. *New Straits Times* [Life & Times section], (p. 7).

Syed Adam Aljafri. (1992). *Ollie's search for golden hope & other stories*. Singapore: Heinemann Asia.

————. (1996). *Reminiscences*. Singapore: Heinemann Asia Ltd.

Tunku Halim Abdullah. (1997). *Dark demon rising.* Petaling Jaya: Pelanduk Publication.

———. (2001).*Vermillion eye.* Petaling Jaya: Pelanduk Publications.

Yahp, B. (1992). *The crocodile fury.* Singapore: Heinemann Asia.

Primary Texts: Non-Fictional

Amir Muhammad *et.al.* (1998). *Generation.* Kuala Lumpur: Hikayat Press.

Chong, S. C. (2001). *Stories for my mother: 1ˢᵗ collection.* Petaling Jaya: Corpcom Services.

Karim Raslan. (1996). *Ceritalah 1.* Singapore: Times Books International

———. (1998). *Heroes & other stories.* Singapore: Zines Books International.

Lee, S. K. (1996). *Malaysian flavours.* Petaling Jaya: Pelanduk Publications.

Marina Mahathir. (1997). *In liberal doses.* Kuala Lumpur: Archipelago Press.

Rehman Rashid. (1993). *A Malaysian journey.* Petaling Jaya: Author.

Secondary Texts

Fanon, F. (1990). *The wretched of the earth.* (3ʳᵈ ed.). (C. Farrington, Trans.). Harmondsworth: Penguin.

Kee, T. C. (December 23, 1992). No first prize winner again this year (on *NST*-Shell poetry competition). *New Straits Times* [Lifestyle / Literary section], (p. 32).

———. (May 5, 1993). Judges award only consolation prizes (on *NST*-Shell poetry competition). *New Straits Times*, (p. 29).

———. (1993, September 15). Seasoned writers win the top prizes (on *NST*-ESSO playwriting competition) in *New Straits Times*, (p. 33.)

Quayum, M. A. & Wicks, P. (eds.). (2001). *Malaysian literature in English: A critical reader.* Petaling Jaya: Pearson Education.

Nor Faridah Abdul Manaf & Quayum, M. A. (2001). *Colonial to global: Malaysian women's writing in English 1940s–1990s.* Kuala Lumpur: International Islamic University Malaysia (IIUM) Press.

Suggested Reading
Chuah Guat Eng
Tan, G. E. (August 24, 1994). Searching for self through writing. *New Straits Times*, (p. 32).

Baldinger, A. (1997, October 29). An echo from the West. *New Straits Times*, (p. 10).

Chin, W.P. (2001). *The mystery of the postcolonial woman.*Working Papers Series. Department of Sociology, University of Singapore.

Che Husna Azhari
Hazidi Hj. Abdul Hamid. (2003). Self, society and the Kelantanese mind: A reading of Che Husna Azhari's Melor in perspective. In Raihanah Mohd. Mydin & Shahrizah Ismail @ Hamdan (eds.), *Linking literacy identities: Malaysian society, culture and the other* (n.p). Serdang: Unversiti Putra Malaysia.

Fadillah Merican. (2000). Going native and staying strong: Malaysian fiction in English. In Halimah Mohd. Said & K. S. Ng (eds.), *English is an Asian language, the Malaysian context* (pp. 107–124). Kuala Lumpur: Persatuan Bahasa Moden Malaysia & The Macquarie Library Pty. Ltd.

Fadillah Merican. (2001). Malay women in Malaysian fiction in English of the 1990s. Seen and Heard. In Fadillah Merican and Ruzy Hashim (eds.), *Native Texts & Contexts: Essays with postcolonial perspectives. A festchrift in honour of Professor Zawiah Yahya* (pp. 55–98). Bangi, Selangor: Fakulti Pengajian Bahasa, Universiti Kebangsaan Malaysia.

About the Authors

Fadillah Merican holds a B.A. (Hons) from the University of Auckland, New Zealand, an M.A. from Victoria University, Wellington, New Zealand, a Diploma of Education from University Malaya and a Ph.D. from the University of Hull, United Kingdom. She was Associate Professor of Literature in English at the School of Language Studies & Linguistics, Universiti Kebangsaan Malaysia (until her retirement in 2003.)

Her publications include *Native Texts and Contexts: Essays with Postcolonial Perspectives* (2001).

Ruzy Suliza Hashim holds a B.A. (Hons) from the University of Otago. She later received an M.A. in Sociology of Literature from University of Essex and a Ph.D. from University of Otago. She is now Associate Professor of Literature at the School of Language Studies and Linguistics, Universiti Kebangsaan Malaysia.

Her publications include *Native Texts and Contexts: Essays with Postcolonial Perspectives* (2001), *Reclaiming Places and Space: Issues in New Literatures* (2003) and *Out of the Shadows: Women in Malay Court Narratives* (2003).

Ganakumaran Subramaniam received his B. Ed (TESL) (Hons) from Universiti Pertanian (Putra) Malaysia. He also holds a masters and Ph.D. in Arts from the University of Nottingham. Currently he serves as a lecturer at the School of Language Studies and Linguistics, Faculty of Social Sciences and Humanities, Universiti Kebangsaan Malaysia. He was also the recipient of the Fulbright Award in the year 2002.

His publications among others include the books; *Teaching of Literature in the ESL/EFL Contexts* (2003) and *Reclaiming Places and Space: Issues in New Literatures* (2003).

Raihanah Mohd Mydin holds a B. Ed (Hons) from Plymouth and an M.A. in Comparative Literature from Universiti Kebangsaan Malaysia. She is now pursuing her Ph.D. at the University of Malaya, looking at the construction of identity in Malaysian Literature in English.

She has published a number of articles in journals and books on issues concerning construction of identity in literary texts. Her latest publication includes *Linking Literary Identities: Malaysian Society, Culture and the Other* (2003) published by Universiti Putra Malaysia Press.